A Practical Guide to Fedora™ and Red Hat® Enterprise Linux®, Sixth Edition

Lab Manual

Mark G. Sobell

PRENTICE HALL

Upper Saddle River, NJ • Boston • Indianapolis • San Francisco
New York • Toronto • Montreal • London • Munich • Paris • Madrid
Capetown • Sydney • Tokyo • Singapore • Mexico City

The publisher offers excellent discounts on this book when ordered in quantity for bulk purchases or special sales, which may include electronic versions and/or custom covers and content particular to your business, training goals, marketing focus, and branding interests. For more information, please contact:

U.S. Corporate and Government Sales
(800) 382-3419
corpsales@pearsontechgroup.com

For sales outside the United States, please contact:

International Sales
international@pearson.com

Visit us on the Web: informit.com/ph

ISBN-13 (print):   978-0-13-290037-9
ISBN-10 (print):   0-13-290037-8
ISBN-13 (PDF):   978-0-13-275735-5
ISBN-10 (PDF):   0-13-275735-4

Print version printed in the United States on recycled paper at Edwards Brothers Malloy in Ann Arbor, Michigan. Third printing, May 2012

Please send comments and corrections to the author at mgs@sobell.com.

Table of Contents

How to Use This Lab Manual

This lab manual is designed for use with Mark Sobell's *A Practical Guide to Fedora and Red Hat Enterprise Linux*, *Sixth Edition*. It contains exercises that correspond to 21 of the book's 28 chapters.

This lab manual has students work on a system on which they install Fedora 15 (the *student-installed system*). The student-installed system can be a standalone physical system or a virtual system running on any platform. The labs are written assuming the student is working in a virtual environment using VMWare Player or Oracle VirtualBox.

Hardware and Software Requirements:

- A system (physical or virtual) for the student-installed system. The system must have at least 1GB of RAM and 20GB of free disk space. The Chapter 3 labs guide the student through setting up this system.

- A system (physical or virtual) for the classroom server. The system must have at least 768MB of RAM and 5GB of free disk space. This system can be installed by the student, provided by the instructor, or in some cases shared by the class. This system is described below.

- The Fedora 15 install DVD from the back of the hardcopy version of the Sobell text or a copy of the Fedora 15 install DVD ISO image file must be available on the student-installed system. If you wish to use a version of Fedora 15 other than the 32bit Intel version, you need to download the ISO image file.

- 3.5GB of free space on the host if you are using the Fedora DVD ISO image file (not the DVD).

Additional Requirements:

A few labs require access to RPM packages not included on the install DVD. These packages can be installed directly if the student-installed system has Internet access, or they can be downloaded in advance and made available to the student-installed system on removable media.

The packages that are required but not included on the Fedora 15 install DVD are:

- autofs
- openldap-servers
- samba-swat
- dhcp

These packages can be downloaded from http://download.fedoraproject.org, which will redirect to a mirror site. Navigate to the **releases/15/Fedora/i386/os/Packages** directory (replace i386 if you are using a different architecture). Download these packages to the student-installed system.

Additionally, a source code tarball will be required. The labs recommend:

- ftp://ftp.gnu.org/gnu/which/

Download this file to the student-installed system.

THE CLASSROOM SERVER:

Many lab exercises require the student-installed systems to have access to a *classroom server*. Instructors can use the provided Kickstart file to build the classroom server. If the classroom server is to be shared by the class, all student-installed systems must have access both *to* and *from* the server (they must be on the same network). If student-installed systems are installed in a Host-Only or NAT configured virtual machine, the classroom server must be installed on that same host. Chapter 3, Lab 4 can be used to install this server or the instructor might provide an pre-installed image.

NETWORK CONSIDERATIONS:

These labs are written with the assumption that both the student-installed system and the classroom server have static addresses in the 172.18.0.0/24 network. The classroom server also offers name services for the example.com domain using addresses in the 172.18.0.0/24 network. If these addresses conflict with your environment, your instructor or network administrator will need to give you alternate network configuration information.

CHAPTER 3, LAB 1: PREPARATION OF THE VIRTUAL ENVIRONMENT OPTION 1: VMWARE PLAYER (10–15 MINUTES)

LEARNING OBJECTIVES AND OUTCOMES:

In this lab, you will obtain installation media and prepare the VMware instance for the initial installation of Linux. These steps are specific to installing under VMware and will end with the Fedora installation Welcome screen, which could otherwise be initiated by booting a new system using the installation DVD.

REQUIRED SETUP AND TOOLS:

- VMware 3.1.4

- Fedora 15 installation DVD

- 25GB free disk space (USB external hard disk)

RECOMMENDED PROCEDURES:

1. Create a new virtual machine for the Fedora installation.

   a. Launch VMware Player.

   b. Choose **Create a New Virtual Machine**.

   c. Choose **I will install the operating system later** and click **Next**.

   d. Select **Linux** and **Fedora** as the Guest Operating System.

   e. IMPORTANT: *Do not* save your image on the shared lab machine. Change the location of the image to specify your USB external hard disk. You may also customize the name of the virtual machine. The default name is Fedora. Customize the name to include your name or initials.

   f. Accept the default of 20GB disk size.

   g. Click **Finish** and if a message about installing VMware Tools appears, click **Close** to return to the VMware Player.

2. To use VMware Player to access the Fedora 15 installation media, select the name of the Fedora image and click **Edit Virtual Machine settings**.

   a. Click **CD/DVD** and specify the location of the Fedora 15 installation DVD.

   b. Click **Advanced** and then place a tick in the check box labeled **Legacy emulation**. Click **OK** to return to the Machine settings page.

   c. Click **OK** to save the settings.

3. To start the installation, select the name of the image and click **Play**.

4. Press CONTROL-G to direct input to the virtual machine. (Press this key to make selections during the installation so that what you type goes to the virtual machine and not to the Windows desktop.)

5. When you see the install DVD Welcome menu (Sobell, page 57) at the beginning of the installation process, press the SPACE bar to pause the countdown. Continue the installation in Chapter 3, Lab 2.

6. Press CONTROL-ALT to return the Windows desktop.

The next installation steps are the same whether installing to a physical or virtual machine.

DELIVERABLES:

The install DVD Welcome menu of the Fedora 15 installation should be visible.

SOLUTIONS:

None

Chapter 3, Lab 1: Preparation of the Virtual Environment
Option 2: Oracle VM VirtualBox (10–15 minutes)

Learning Objectives and Outcomes:

In this lab you will obtain installation media and prepare the VirtualBox instance for the initial installation of Linux. These steps are specific to installing in VirtualBox and will end with the Fedora installation welcome screen, which could otherwise be initiated by booting a new system using the installation DVD.

Required Setup and Tools:

- Oracle VM VirtualBox 4.0

- Fedora 15 installation DVD

- 25GB free disk space (USB external hard disk)

Recommended Procedures:

1. Create a new virtual machine for the Fedora installation.

    a. Launch VirtualBox.

    b. Click **New** to launch the Create New Virtual Machine wizard and then click **Next**.

    c. Name the virtual machine **Fedora-*name*** where ***name*** is your name or initials. Then select Linux as the operating system and Fedora as the version. Click **Next** after making all changes.

    d. Allocate 1,024MB of memory for the Virtual Machine and click **Next**.

    e. Accept the default of Create new hard disk and then click **Next**.

    f. After starting the Create new Virtual Disk wizards, keep the default Dynamically expanding storage or change to Fixed-size storage as specified by your instructor. Then click **Next**. (Note: The Fixed-size option might take a long time to allocate space. If you use the Dynamically expanding option, make sure you do not run out of space on your external hard drive before the end of the course.)

    g. IMPORTANT: *Do not* store your new virtual machine image on a shared lab machine. Change the location that you store your virtual machine to your USB external hard disk. Change the size of the disk to 20GB and then click **Next**.

    h. After reviewing the setup, click **Finish** to create the storage device and then click **Finish** again to create the virtual machine.

2. To use Virtual Box to access the Fedora 15 installation DVD, select the name of the Fedora installation DVD and click **Settings**.

    a. Click **Storage** on the left, click the **Add CD/DVD** icon (the disk with the plus sign over it), click **Choose Disk**, and specify the location of the Fedora 15 installation DVD.

    b. Click **OK** to save the settings.

3. To start the installation, select the name of the image and click **Start**.

4. Press the *right* CONTROL key or click the mouse in the virtual machine window to direct input to the virtual machine. (Press this key while you are installing the image so what you type goes to the virtual machine and not to the Windows desktop.)

5. When you see the install DVD Welcome menu (Sobell, page 57) at the beginning of the installation process, press the SPACE bar to pause the countdown. Continue the installation in Chapter 3, Lab 2.

6. Press the *right* CONTROL key to return the Windows desktop.

The next installation steps are the same whether you are installing on a physical or virtual machine.

DELIVERABLES:

The install DVD Welcome menu should be visible (Sobell, page 57).

SOLUTIONS:

None

CHAPTER 3, LAB 1: PREPARATION OF THE VIRTUAL ENVIRONMENT OPTION 3: A STANDALONE PHYSICAL SYSTEM (10–15 MINUTES)

WARNINGS:

- There is no information provided in these labs for a configuring dual boot system (Sobell, page 82).

- You are about to remove all information from the hard disk of this machine. *You will lose all data on the machine.*

- When you get to Chapter 3, Lab 2, be sure to remove all partitions rather than just replacing the Linux partitions.

- You will need to obtain the following information from your instructor or network administrator

  - hostname

  - IP address

  - netmask

  - router

  - nameserver

- You will need to substitute new values for these items throughout the labs.

- You will need a second (physical) machine for the classroom server. Your instructor may provide this machine as a shared system for the class.

RECOMMENDED PROCEDURE:

1. Place the installation DVD in the drive

2. Boot the machine.

3. When you see the install DVD Welcome menu (Sobell, page 57) at the beginning of the installation process, press the SPACE bar to pause the countdown.

4. Continue with Chapter 3, Lab 2.

DELIVERABLES:

The install DVD Welcome menu should be visible (Sobell, page 57).

SOLUTIONS:

None

CHAPTER 3, LAB 2: INSTALLING FEDORA 15 (30–50 MINUTES)

LEARNING OBJECTIVES AND OUTCOMES:

You should be able to work through the Anaconda installation questions to complete a Fedora 15 installation from installation DVD, customizing partitioning and software selection. If you are installing on a virtual system using VMWare or VirtualBox, or if you are installing on a physical system, this lab continues where the Chapter 3, Lab 1 left off.

REQUIRED SETUP AND TOOLS:

- A physical or virtual system booted from the Fedora 15 installation DVD or the DVD ISO image and displaying the install DVD Welcome menu (Sobell, page 57)

ADDITIONAL RESOURCES:

- Sobell, Chapter 3

- Installation Guide, Chapter 8, at docs.fedoraproject.org

RECOMMENDED PROCEDURES:

Install Fedora 15 as a mail server with a graphical desktop. Use the following specific requirements:

- Set the hostname to **linux.example.com.**

- Set the root password to **P@$$w0rd**.

- Customize the network settings to Connect automatically.

- Include a 500MB /boot physical partition. Use the remaining space for an LVM partition that contains a 1024MB swap logical volume, a 256MB /home logical volume, and a 16GB / (root) logical volume. Leave any remaining space unused (free).

- Install the system as a Graphical Desktop and Customize Now. During installation, install a Mail Server and click **Development** in the left pane of the package selection screen (Sobell, page 65) and then click **Development Tools** in the right pane to install the compilers VMware Tools requires.

- Set the language, keyboard, and time zone to your location.

- Unless otherwise noted, accept the defaults.

DETAILED STEPS:

If you have not already booted your (physical or virtual) system using the Fedora 15 installation DVD, insert (or attach) the media and boot the system. If you are using VMWare Player, start with Chapter 3, Lab 1 and continue here.

Beginning with the install DVD Welcome menu (Sobell, page 57)

1. Use the ARROW keys to highlight **Install a new system or upgrade an existing system** and press RETURN to begin the installation.

2. Test your media (Sobell, "The Disc Found Screen," page 57). If you have tested this installation disk previously, skip this step.

3. Select a language and then a keyboard (Sobell, page 59).

4. Accept the default for Basic Storage Devices.

5. If asked, initialize the drive by clicking **Yes, discard any data** (Sobell, page 60). Also, if asked, perform a Fresh Installation (Sobell, pages 34 and 60).

6. Set the hostname to **linux.example.com** and Configure Network to Connect Automatically (Sobell, Network Connections Window, page 653).

   a. Click **Configure Network**.

   b. Click the name of the wired network to select and then click **Edit**.

   c. Put a tick in the check box labeled **Connect automatically** and click **Save**.

   d. Click **Close** to return to the installation.

7. Select the appropriate time zone for your location.

8. Set the root password to **P@$$w0rd** and accept the use of a weak password.

9. Choose the default to Replace Existing Linux System(s). Make sure the check box labeled **Review and modify partitioning layout** at the bottom left of the screen has a tick in it.

10. Modify the partitioning (Sobell, page 71)

    a. Highlight the line with a type of swap and then click **Edit**.

    b. In the Edit Logical Volume window, set the size to 1024MB and then click **OK**.

    c. Highlight the line with the device named Free and click **Create**.

       i. In the Create Storage window select **LVM Logical Volume** and click **Create**.

       ii. In the Make Logical Volume window specify the Mount Point as /home.

       iii. Ensure the filesystem type is ext4.

       iv. Set the size to 256MB.

       v. Click **OK**.

    d. Highlight the line with a Mount Point of **/** and click **Edit**.

    e. Adjust the size to 16384 and then click **OK**.

11. Click **Next** and then select **Format** from the Format Warnings window. When asked to confirm, click **Write Changes to Disk**.

12. Accept the defaults for the Boot Loader.

13. Leave the default of Graphical Desktop. Do not add any additional repositories. Ensure that **Customize Now** at the bottom of the screen is selected.

14. In the package selection screen (Sobell, page 64), ensure that Mail Server is installed: Select **Servers** in the left pane and add a tick to **Mail Server** in the right pane. Also click **Development** in the left pane and **Development Tools** in the right pane to install the compilers necessary for installing VMware Tools.

15. Click **Next** and wait for the files to copy and the screen to prompt for a reboot.

DELIVERABLES:

A completed installation ready to reboot and perform initial configuration at Firstboot. Continue with Chapter 3, Lab 3.

SOLUTIONS:

None

Chapter 3, Lab 3: Firstboot (5–10 minutes)

Learning Objectives and Outcomes:

The final stage of a Fedora 15 installation is named Firstboot; it customizes the system with an initial user and the date, time, and time zone. When complete, log in on the graphical desktop using your newly created account.

Note: In this lab you will add the user named **student**.

Required Setup and Tools:

- A Fedora 15 installation prompting to reboot at the end of the installation (continued from Chapter 3, Lab 2)

Additional Resources:

- Sobell, Chapter 3, Firstboot, page 65

- Installation Guide, Chapter 16, at docs.fedoraproject.org

Recommended Procedures:

Complete the installation to meet the following requirements:

1. Create a local, ordinary (*not* administrator) user account for **Sammy Student** with a username of **student** and a password of **P@$$w0rd**.

2. Verify the date and time.

3. Do not send a hardware profile. (Sobell, page 66)

4. Unless otherwise noted, accept all defaults.

Once the initial configuration is completed, log into the graphical desktop as the user named **student**.

Detailed Steps:

1. If your system is displaying the **Congratulations, your Fedora installation is complete** screen at the end of the installation, click **Reboot** to reboot the system. Fedora reboots and displays the Welcome screen (Sobell, page 66).

2. Click **Forward** on the Welcome screen.

3. Click **Forward** to acknowledge the License Information.

4. Create a local, ordinary user (*not* an administrator account) with

   a. Full Name: **Sammy Student**

   b. Username: **student**

   c. Password: **P@$$w0rd**

   d. Do not change any other settings. Click **Forward**.

5. Verify the date and time and adjust as necessary. Click **Forward**.

6. Accept the default of **Do not send profile** and then click **Finish** and **No, do not send** when asked to reconsider (Sobell, page 66).

7. Log in as the user named **student**.

8. If GNOME3 fails to load, accept the Fallback mode by clicking **Close**. If the desktop starts without displaying any errors, follow the steps on Sobell, page 92, to force your system to log you in in Fallback mode, log out, and log back in to put the system in Fallback mode.

DELIVERABLES:

A Fedora 15 desktop running in Fallback mode for the user named **student**.

SOLUTIONS:

None

CHAPTER 3, LAB 4: INSTALLING FEDORA USING KICKSTART (15–30 MINUTES)

LEARNING OBJECTIVES AND OUTCOMES:

Perform an unattended installation of Fedora 15 using an existing Kickstart file. You can use this lab to set up the classroom server.

REQUIRED SETUP AND TOOLS:

- A new virtual machine with 5GB of disk space on the same host as your linux.example.com virtual machine. Or a new physical machine on the same network as your linux.example.com machine.

- A copy of the Fedora installation DVD or DVD ISO image file (used to install the required packages).

- Access to the Classroom Server Kickstart file (URL provided by your instructor).

ADDITIONAL RESOURCES:

- Sobell, Chapter 2

- Sobell, Chapter 3

RECOMMENDED PROCEDURES:

1. Start your installation as explained in Chapter 3, Lab 1.

2. At the install DVD Welcome menu (Sobell, page 57), press the TAB key to modify the boot parameters (Sobell, page 68, Figure 3-13).

3. Add an argument of **ks=*URL*** where *URL* is the location of the Kickstart file. For example, **ks=http://school.net/~instructor/class-server.ks.cfg**

4. When the system reboots, log in as **max** with a password of **P@$$w0rd** to verify the installation. The command **hostname** should return server.example.com.

5. You may shut down the new system until it is needed later for other labs.

DELIVERABLES:

An classroom server for use in other labs.

SOLUTIONS:

None

Chapter 4, Lab 1: Customizing and Adding Users to Your New System (20–30 minutes)

Learning Objectives and Outcomes:

This lab explores a newly installed system using graphical tools. You will launch applications to preview later chapters in the text as you add users and view network and disk information. You will also have an opportunity to verify the customization done at install time and, if you are using VMWare, follow a procedure to install VMware Tools.

Note: In this lab you will add the users named **mark** and **max** as well as the group named **linux**. The users named **mark** and **max** will belong to the group named **linux**.

Required Setup and Tools:

- A Running Fedora 15 system (the result of Chapter 3, Lab 3) with passwords for an ordinary user (student) and root

- The graphical desktop

Additional Resources:

- Sobell, Chapter 4, page 109, Updating Software

- Sobell, Chapter 16, page 602, system-config-users

- Sobell, Chapter 11, page 413, Using su to Gain root Privileges

- Sobell, Chapter 11, page 475, Table 11-4, Graphical Configuration Tools

- Deployment Guide, Section 3.2 at docs.fedoraproject.org

Recommended Procedures:

1. Disable automatic updates (Sobell, page 123).

   a. Select ApplicationsàOtheràSoftware Updates

   b. Change the **Automatically install** to **Nothing**.

   c. Click **Close** to save the new settings.

2. Verify network connectivity.

   a. Determine the IP Address of the newly installed system by right clicking the Network Icon (two computers) in the upper-right corner of the screen and then clicking **Connection Information**. Make a note of your IP address 192.168.100.83 and the Default Route 192.168.100.2

   b. Open a virtual terminal displaying a command-line prompt by selecting ApplicationsàSystem ToolsàTerminal.

c. Ping the default route using the command **ping -c3 *IP*** where *IP* is the IP address of the router as recorded in Step 2a (preceding). The **-c3** option causes the ping utility to issue three pings and then quits.

d. Enter **exit** and press RETURN to close the virtual terminal.

3. Add users and groups to the system.

a. Select ApplicationsàOtheràUsers and Groups to open the User Manager window (Sobell, page 602). Enter the root password when prompted.

b. Click the **Add User** icon and fill in the fields to add the user **max** with a password of **P@$$w0rd**.

c. Click **Add User** again to add the user **mark** with a password of **P@$$w0rd**.

d. Add a user of your choosing with a password you will remember.

e. Click the **Add Group** icon to add a group named **linux**.

4. Add users to a group. In the User Manager window, add the users named **max** and **mark** to the group named **linux**.

a. Click the **Groups** tab.

b. Highlight the **linux** group.

c. Click the **Properties** icon.

d. Click the **Group Users** tab.

e. Scroll down and add ticks to the boxes labeled **mark** and **max**.

f. Click **OK** to complete the modifications.

5. VMWARE USERS ONLY: Install VMware Tools to improve performance of hardware devices (mouse, sound, etc.) in the VMware environment. Note: Follow these steps as specified. Over the course of the class, you will learn more about each of the commands issued here.

a. From your host desktop in the VMware Player application, click **Virtual Machine** and then Install **VMware Tools**. Accept all prompts to download and install. This installation process copies the required files to the Fedora machine. When VMPlayer indicates the install has completed, return to the Fedora desktop and continue extracting the tools.

b. From the Fedora desktop, select ApplicationsàSystem ToolsàTerminal to open a virtual terminal displaying a command-line prompt.

c. At the command prompt, gain root privileges by typing **su –** and then entering the root password at the prompt.

d. Working with root privileges, extract the VMware Tools installation files using the command **tar xvf /media/VMware\ Tools/VMwareTools*.tar.gz**

e. Working with root privileges, type the command **/root/VMware Tools-distrib/VMware-install.pl** and press RETURN to accept the defaults for all prompts. The compilation and attempt to start VMware Tools will take up to several minutes and will display messages on the screen as it proceeds. When it is complete, the shell will display a command prompt.

f. Reboot the system by typing **reboot** and pressing RETURN at the command prompt or by clicking the *username* in the upper right corner and then selecting **Shut Down** and **Restart**.

g. After the system reboots, log in and verify that VMware Tools is installed by opening a terminal window and typing **ps -ef | grep vmware**; this command should show vmware-user running. Another option is to run **vmware-toolbox**.

6. Optional: Additional exploration of installation settings.

a. View disk partitioning information by selecting ApplicationsàAccessoriesàDisk Utility. Look at the items under Multi Disk devices; you should be able to verify the size of the swap, /home, and / (root) logical devices.

b. Change the date and time settings, including the time zone, by selecting ApplicationsàOtheràDate & Time. Supply the root password when prompted.

c. Change the systemwide language setting by selecting ApplicationsàOtheràLanguage. Enter the root password when prompted. A user may also change her own desktop language settings by selecting ApplicationsàSystem ToolsàSystem Settings and then clicking the **Region and Language** icon.

DELIVERABLES:

Three new user accounts (**max, mark,** and a user of your choosing) plus one new group account (**linux**); **max** and **mark** belong to the **linux** group.

SOLUTIONS:

None

CHAPTER 5, LAB 1: COMMON LINUX COMMANDS (30–40 MINUTES)

LEARNING OBJECTIVES AND OUTCOMES:

You should become comfortable using the Linux command line to browse the filesystem, determine the type of a file, display text files, and use the online help utilities.

REQUIRED SETUP AND TOOLS:

- Fedora Linux 15 installation with an ordinary user (student)

ADDITIONAL RESOURCES:

- Sobell, Chapter 4, man (page 126) and info (page 128)

- Sobell, Chapter 5, page 149, basic utilities including less

- Sobell, Chapter 6, Important Files (page 199) and absolute/relative pathnames (page 191)

RECOMMENDED PROCEDURES:

All commands can be given from the command-line interface displayed by a terminal emulator in the graphical environment. To open a terminal emulator window select Applications System Tools Terminal.

Commands can include options and arguments. Options modify the behavior of the command; arguments provide data used by the command. Many commands can be run without any options or arguments, with only options or arguments, or with both options and arguments (Sobell, Command Line, page 226).

1. Try giving the following commands and observe the behavior with each combination of options and arguments.

   a. List the names of the files in the working directory.

      ls ~~list directory contents~~

   b. By default, **ls** does not list files that have hidden filenames (filenames that begin with a period; Sobell, page 190). List the names of all files in the working directory, including those with hidden filenames.

      ls -a ~~all contents~~

   c. Each file has an owner, size, modification date, and permissions. Show these characteristics for all files in the working directory.

      ls -l ~~use a long listing format~~

   d. By default, **ls** lists the files in the working directory. Instead, list the contents of the /tmp directory by specifying that directory as an argument to **ls**.

      ls /tmp ~~tmp filled with a comma append indicator~~

   e. List the contents of both the /tmp directory and the /var directory. List files and directories that have hidden filenames and show the ownership of each file.

      ls -al /tmp /var ~~gdm, tmp~~

2. Which utility can you use to display the absolute pathname of the working directory? What is the absolute pathname of the working directory?

pwd

3. Change directories so the /tmp directory is the working directory and verify the name of the working directory.

cd /tmp
pwd

4. What is the quickest way to make your home directory the working directory?

cd

5. Explore the important standard directories and files listed at Sobell, pages 199-201. Make use of **cd**, **ls**, and **pwd** (Sobell, pages 196, 202, and 190, respectively) and absolute and relative pathnames (Sobell, page 192).

   a. Use an absolute pathname to make the directory that contains system log files the working directory.
   cd /var/log

   b. Use an absolute pathname to make your home directory the working directory.
   cd /home/student

   c. Starting with your home directory as the working directory, use a relative pathname to make the /etc directory the working directory.
   cd ../../etc

   d. Starting with the /etc/ directory as the working directory, use a relative pathname to list the contents of the directory that contains the configuration files for the X window system.
   ls X11

6. Linux does not rely on filenames or filename extensions to determine the type of a file. Use the **file** utility (Sobell, page 156) to determine the type of the following files.

   a. /etc/passwd   *ASCII text*

   b. /usr/bin/passwd   *exeutable*

   c. /var/log   *directory*

   d. /usr/share/man/man1/ls.1.gz   *gzip compressed data*

   e. /dev/tty1   *character special*

   f. /dev/sda1   *block special*

   g. /dev/cdrom   *symbolic link*

h. /usr/share/magic   *symbolic link*

i. /usr/share/pixmaps/faces/sky.jpg   *jpg image*

7. Text files can be viewed using **cat**, **head**, **tail**, and **less** (Sobell, pages 148, 152, 153, and 149, respectively). Choose the best application to

   a. Display the contents of the /etc/issue file.

   cat /etc/issue

   b. Display the contents of the /etc/sysconfig/network file.

   cat /etc/network

   c. Display the first few lines of the /etc/passwd file.

   head /etc/passwd

   d. Determine the last word in the /usr/share/dict/linux.words file.

   tail /usr/share/dict/linux.words

   e. Display the /etc/profile file.

   less /etc/profile

8. Display the /etc/passwd file using **less**.

   less /etc/passwd

   a. Jump to end by giving the command **G**.

   b. Search for mark by giving the command **/mark**.

   c. Jump to top by giving the command **g**.

   d. Search for bash by giving the command **/bash**.

   e. Find the next occurrence of bash by giving the command **n**.

   f. Quit by giving the command **q**.

9. Use **man** and **info**.

   a. Which **ls** option sorts the output by modification time?

   ls -lt /etc

   b. Which **head** option displays the first 5 lines of a file instead of the default 10 lines?

   head -n 5 /etc/passwd

   c. Which **tail** option continues to display a file as additional content is added to the file (such as watching a log file)? (Hint: Search for *follow*.)

   tail -f /var/log/message

   d. Which **cal** option displays three months instead of the default current month?

   cal -3

e. Use **whatis** to see which man pages relate to **passwd**.

> *whatis passwd*

f. Display the man page for the file named passwd (not the utility).

> *man 5passwd*

g. Use **man -k** (apropos) to find a utility that shows who is logged in on the system.

> *man -k who*

h. Which command reports on free disk space? (Tip: When you want to search for a string with a space, put quotation marks around it: "disk space".)

> *man -k disk space df*

i. The end of the man page for **df** has a SEE ALSO referencing **info**. Explore the **df** info page.

> *info 'coreutils' df invocation*

10. Optional: Learn more about using the **info** utility by reading the info page on info. (Give the command **info info**.)

DELIVERABLES:

A better understanding of issuing commands from the Linux command prompt.

CHAPTER 5, LAB 1—SOLUTIONS:

1. n/a

2. Which utility can you use to display the absolute pathname of the working directory? What is the absolute pathname of the working directory?

    pwd

    varies depending on your username

3. Change directories so the /tmp directory is the working directory and verify the name of the working directory.

    cd /tmp

    pwd

4. What is the quickest way to make your home directory the working directory?

    cd

5. n/a

6. Linux does not rely on filenames or filename extensions to determine the type of a file. Use the **file** utility (Sobell, page 156) to determine the type of the following files.

    a. /etc/passwd: ASCII text

    b. /usr/bin/passwd: executable

    c. /var/log: directory

    d. /usr/share/man/man1/ls.1.gz: gzip compressed data

    e. /dev/tty1:   character special

    f. /dev/sda: block special

    g. /dev/cdrom: symbolic link

    h. /usr/share/magic: symbolic link

    i. /usr/share/pixmaps/faces/sky.png: JPEG image data

7. Text files can be viewed using **cat, head, tail,** and **less** (Sobell, pages 148, 152, 153, and 149, respectively). Choose the best application to

    a. Display the contents of the /etc/issue file.

       cat /etc/issue

    b. Display the contents of the /etc/sysconfig/network file.

       cat /etc/sysconfig/network

    c. Display the first few lines of the /etc/passwd file.

       head /etc/passwd

    d. Determine the last word in the /usr/share/dict/linux.words file.

    tail /usr/share/dict/linux.words

    e. Display the /etc/profile file.

    less /etc/profile (Hint: Use q to quit less.)

8. n/a

9. Use man and info.

    a. Which **ls** option sorts the output by modification time?

    ls -lt /etc

    b. Which **head** option displays the first 5 lines of a file instead of the default 10 lines?

    head -n 5 /etc/passwd

    c. Which **tail** option continues to display a file as additional content is added to the file (such as watching a log file)? (Hint: Search for *follow*.)

    tail -f /var/log/messages

    d. Which **cal** option displays three months instead of the default current month?

    cal -3

    e. Use **whatis** to see which man pages relate to **passwd**.

    whatis passwd

    f. Display the man page for the file named passwd (not the utility).

    man 5 passwd

    g. Use **man -k** (apropos) to find a utility that shows who is logged in on the system.

    man -k who

    h. Which command reports on free disk space? (Tip: When you want to search for a string with a space, put quotation marks around it: "disk space".)

    man -k "disk space"

    df

    i. The end of the man page for **df** has a SEE ALSO referencing info. Explore the **df** info page.

    info coreutils 'df invocation'

10. n/a

Chapter 5, Lab 2: Editing Text Files (30–40 minutes)

Learning Objectives and Outcomes:

You will become comfortable using various text editors in the Linux operating system.

Required Setup and Tools:

- Fedora Linux 15 installation with an ordinary user (student) and the root password

Additional Resources:

- Sobell, Chapter 5, page 172, vim tutorial

Recommended Procedures:

Each Linux distribution includes several text editors. The default graphical editor with the GNOME desktop is gedit and with KDE is kedit. Both are similar in features to Notepad or WordPad. If the graphical environment is not available, you can use nano, a simple editor that is similar to DOSEdit. Advanced editing, including cut and paste, search and replace, and applying filters in the text environment, can be performed using vi (vim) or emacs.

Part I: Explore gedit and nano before focusing on the VI Enhanced (vim) editor.

1. Create a new file using **gedit**.

    a. Open gedit by selecting Applicationsà Accessoriesà gedit Text Editor.

    b. Add the text **This file is being created using gedit.**

    c. Save the file with the name **practice.txt**.

    d. Return to the command line and use **ls** to view the ownership and **file** to determine the type of file. Note: **gedit** does not automatically add any filename extensions. If you want the file named practice.txt, you must specify that entire name when saving the file.

2. Modify the same file using **nano**.

    a. From the command line type **nano practice.txt**.

    b. Use the ARROW keys to place the cursor at the end of the file.

    c. Add a line of additional text: "This file was then edited using nano."

    d. Save the file by giving the command CONTROL-O (write out). Press RETURN to keep the same filename.

    e. Exit nano by giving the command CONTROL-X (exit).

3. Finally, edit the same file using **vim**.

    a. From the command line type **vim practice.txt**.

b. Use the ARROW keys to place the cursor at the end of the file.

c. Press the INSERT key before typing an additional line of text **This file was then edited using vim** and press ESCAPE when you are finished.

d. Type **:wq** (write and quit) or **ZZ** to save and exit.

The graphical text editors have the advantage of being easy to use, similar to text editors in other operating systems, and of allowing the use of the mouse to highlight text in order to copy, cut, and paste. However, many Linux systems, especially servers, do not have a graphical environment available.

The nano editor is simple and provides prompts at the bottom to assist with common commands such as save and exit. Most commands, however, require you to press the CONTROL key along with one or more other keys; it is limited in what it can do and is not as easy to use for copying and pasting. CONTROL-G displays the online help and CONTROL-W searches within your text file—but does not search while in help.

The vim editor allows for most common keyboard special keys, provides online help that uses the same keys to navigate and search as are used when working with the text file, and is extremely powerful when doing a lot of text manipulation. The commands are fairly simple, but it does take some time to get accustomed to using the different modes.

Part II: Explore the power of vim

4. Copy the /usr/share/dict/words file to your home directory.

   cp /usr/share/dict/words/home/student

5. Open the words file using **vim**.

   vim words

6. Some commands are the same as less and man.

   a. Jump to the end of the document.

   G

   b. Return to the top of the document.

   1G or **gg**

   c. Search for the words that contain the string **learning**.

   /learning

   n finds the next occurrence

   /^learning finds a line that begins with **learning**

7. Any command can be preceded by a number.

   a. Jump to line 150 with **150G**.

   b. Move forward one word using **w** and then seven words using **7w**.

   c. Delete one line using **dd** and then delete three lines using **3dd**.

   d. Move to the beginning of the file using **gg** and paste the three lines at the top of the file using **P**.

e. Challenge: Jump to the line containing **zach** and then delete everything from that line to the end of the file.

/zach

dG

f. Undo the previous command using **u**.

8. Display online help in vim by giving the command **:help**. To leave help and return to your text file, use **:q**.

a. Use help to determine the command to quit all files without saving.

:qa!

b. How do you get additional help on the quit command?

:help quit

c. How do you get help on the / (search) command?

:help /

9. Quit editing the file without saving your changes.

:q!

Part III: Modify the text displayed above a login prompt on a text-based console

The text displayed above a login prompt on a text-based console is generated from the /etc/issue file.

10. Add to the end of the /etc/issue file a line that identifies the purpose of the system: **This system is a lab system for the** *course name* **course and is assigned to** *your name,* replacing *course name* and *your name* with appropriate information.

a. Give the command **su –** to gain root privileges.

b. Give the command **vim /etc/issue** to open the issue file for editing.

c. Use the ARROW keys to move the cursor to the last line in the file.

d. Give the command **o** (lowercase "oh"), use the insert key, or **i** to open a line below the cursor and enter Insert mode.

e. Add the line **This system is a lab system for the** *course name* **course and is assigned to** *your name* modified with your course and name.

f. Press ESCAPE to leave Insert mode and return to Command mode.

g. Type **:wq** or **ZZ** to write and quit.

11. Switch to a text-based terminal to verify that the issue information has been modified. You may have to press RETURN once to see the change.

a. Press SHIFT-CONTROL-ALT-F2 to change to a text-based virtual terminal. For more information on switching virtual terminals (also called virtual consoles) see Sobell page 138 and Chapter 11, Lab 1.

b. Press RETURN to refresh the login prompt.

c. Press SHIFT-CONTROL-ALT-F1 to return to the graphical desktop.

12. Use **man** to discover the meaning of the **\r** and **\m** characters in the /etc/issue file.

    a. **man -k issue** shows there is a man page for issue.

    b. **man issue** describes the purpose of the file and references the \char sequences that are interpreted by the getty programs. The Fedora virtual consoles use mingetty.

    c. **man mingetty** (Tip: If you want to search for the **\r** use, /\\r. Otherwise search for **escape** or press the PAGE DOWN key several times to display the list of escape sequences.)

13. Add the network node name and the current date to your /etc/issue file.

    \n inserts the machines network node name

    \d inserts the current date

14. Optional: Learn more about vim by using vimtutor (Sobell, page 172).

DELIVERABLES:

A modified /etc/issue file.

Chapter 5, Lab 2—SOLUTIONS:

1.–3. n/a

4. Copy the /usr/share/dict/words file to your home directory.

   cp /usr/share/dict/words /home/student/

5. Open the words file using vim.

   vim words

6.–12. n/a

13. Add the network node name and the current date to your /etc/issue file.

   \n inserts the machines network node name.

   \d inserts the current date.

14. n/a

CHAPTER 6, LAB 1: MANAGING FILES (15–25 MINUTES)

LEARNING OBJECTIVES AND OUTCOMES:

You should become comfortable using the Linux command line and the online help utilities to manage files and directories.

REQUIRED SETUP AND TOOLS:

- Fedora Linux 15 installation with an ordinary user (student)

ADDITIONAL RESOURCES:

- Sobell, Chapter 6

- Sobell, Chapter 5

- Sobell, Chapter 4, pages 126 (man) and 128 (info)

RECOMMENDED PROCEDURES:

All commands can be given from the command line by using a terminal emulator in a graphical environment. Open a terminal emulator by selecting ApplicationsàSystem ToolsàTerminal.

1. As an ordinary user such as **student,** create a directory named **Unit2** in your home directory.

   mkdir unit2

2. Create subdirectories under Unit2 named **memos** and **reports.**

   mkdir unit2/memos
   mkdir unit2/reports

3. The **touch** utility updates the time stamp on an existing file or creates a new, empty file with the specified name (man touch). Ensure your home directory is your working directory and then create some files for this exercise using the following commands:

   cd

   touch memo.one

   touch memo.two

   touch memo.three

   touch report.jan report.feb report.mar

4. Copy the memo.one file to the Unit2/memos directory.

   cp memo.onefile unit2/memo directory

5. Copy the memo.two file to the Unit2/memos directory and change the name to memo.2.

   cp memo.two unit2/memos/memo.2

6. Move the memo.three file to the Unit2/memos directory.

   mv memo.three /Unit2/memos

7. Move the three reports to the Unit2/reports directory.

mv report.jan report.feb report.mar Unit2/reports

8. Make the Unit2/reports directory the working directory. Before modifying the report.mar file, make a backup copy of the file with a **.orig** filename extension.

mv reports.jan reports.feb repo

9. Copy the /etc/passwd file to Unit2/reports/report.jan file, overwriting the reports.jan file. Use a **cat** command before and after to verify that you overwrote the file.

cp -i /etc/password report.jan

10. Copy the /etc/hosts file to Unit2/reports/report.feb. Have the utility you use to copy the file ask for confirmation before overwriting report.feb.

cp -i /etc/host/ report.feb

11. Remove the remaining memo files in your home directory.

cd   rm memo.one memo.two

12. Remove the report.jan file. Have the utility you use to remove the file ask for confirmation before removing report.jan.

rm -i Unit2/reports/report.feb.

13. Remove the memos directory, including all files in the directory.

rm -r unit2/memos

14. Use **locate** to find a file that contains the string **chess**.

locate chess

15. Use **locate** to find a file that contains the string **sky**.

locate sky

16. Copy the /usr/share/dict/words file to your home directory.

cp /usr/share/dict/words ~

a. What is the size of the words file?

ls -l word

b. Compress the file using **gzip**. What is the resulting file size?

gzip words

c. Uncompress the file. What is the resulting file size?

gunzip words.zip

d. Compress the file using **bzip2**. What is the resulting file size?

bzip2 words

e. Uncompress the file. What is the resulting file size?

bzip2 words.bz2

17. Optional: Repeat the above compression exercise with other types of files, such as a JPG from the /usr/share/pixmaps/faces directory.

DELIVERABLES:

Files organized in the Unit2 subdirectory.

Chapter 6, Lab 1—Solutions:

1. As an ordinary user such as student, create a directory named **Unit2** in your home directory.
   mkdir Unit2

2. Create subdirectories under Unit2 named **memos** and **reports**.
   mkdir Unit2/memos
   mkdir Unit2/reports
   or:
   cd Unit2
   mkdir memos reports

3. The **touch** utility updates the time stamp on an existing file or creates a new, empty file with the specified name (man touch). Ensure your home directory is your working directory and then create some files for this exercise using the following commands:
   cd
   touch memo.one
   touch memo.two
   touch memo.three
   touch report.jan report.feb report.mar

4. Copy the memo.one file to the Unit2/memos directory.
   cp memo.one Unit2/memos

5. Copy the memo.two file to the Unit2/memos directory and change the name to memo.2.
   cp memo.two Unit2/memos/memo.2

6. Move the memo.three file to the Unit2/memos directory.
   mv memo.three /Unit2/memos

7. Move the three reports to the Unit2/reports directory.
   mv report.jan report.feb report.mar Unit2/reports

8. Make the Unit2/reports directory the working directory. Before modifying the report.mar file, make a backup copy of the file with a **.orig** filename extension.
   cd Unit2/reports
   cp report.mar report.mar.orig

9. Copy the /etc/passwd file to Unit2/reports/report.jan file, overwriting the reports.jan file. Use a cat command before and after to verify that you overwrote the file.
   cp /etc/passwd report.jan

10. Copy the /etc/hosts file to Unit2/reports/report.feb. Have the utility you use to copy the file ask for confirmation before overwriting report.feb.
    cp -i /etc/hosts report.feb

11. Remove the remaining memo files in your home directory.

cd

rm memo.one memo.two

12. Remove the report.jan file having the utility you use to remove the file ask for confirmation before removing report.jan.

rm -i Unit2/reports/report.jan

13. Remove the memos directory including all files in the directory.

rm -r Unit2/memos

or

rm Unit2/memos/memo.one

rm Unit2/memos/memo.2

rm Unit2/memos/memo.three

rmdir Unit2/memos

14. Use locate to find a file that contains the string **chess**.

locate chess

15. Use locate to find a file that contains the string **sky**.

locate sky

16. Copy the /usr/share/dict/words file to your home directory.

cp /usr/share/dict/words ~

    a. What is the size of the words file?

    ls -l words

    b. Compress the file using **gzip**. What is the resulting file size?

    gzip words

    c. Uncompress the file. What is the resulting file size?

    gunzip words.gz

    d. Compress the file using **bzip2**. What is the resulting file size?

    bzip2 words

    e. Uncompress the file. What is the resulting file size?

    bunzip2 words.bz2

17. n/a

Chapter 6, Lab 2: Managing File and Directory Permissions (15–20 minutes)

Learning Objectives and Outcomes:

You will use the Linux command line interface (CLI) and manage file and directory access using file permission settings.

Required Setup and Tools:

- Fedora Linux 15 installation with three ordinary users (student, max, and mark). (Note: The user named **student** is created in Chapter 3, Lab 3, **max** and **mark** are created in Chapter 4, Lab 1; **max** and **mark** should be members of the group named **linux**.)

Additional Resources:

- Sobell, Chapter 6, page 202, access permissions

- man pages

- info pages

Recommended Procedures:

1. Determine the permissions of various files and directories on the system. Fill in the chart below:

Filename	Readable by	Writable by	Executable/ Searchable by	Symbolic Type and Permissions	Octal Permissions
/etc/passwd	Owner (root), group (root), and everyone else	Owner (root)	none	-rw-r--r--	644
/etc/shadow	none	none	none	-------	000
/etc/cups/cupsd.conf	Owner (root) group (lp)	owner(root)	none	-rw-r--	640
/var/log/audit	Owner (root)	Owner(root)	none	-rw----	600
/var/log/cups	Owner (lp) group(sys) everyone else	owner (lp)	owner(lp) group (sys) every one else	drwxr-xr-x	755
/etc/cups/ssl	owner (root)	owner (root)	owner (root)	drwx---	700
/var/spool/mail	owner (root) group (root) and everyone else	owner (root) group (root)	owner(root) group (root) every one else	drw xrwxr-x	755

Filename	Readable by	Writable by	Executable/ Searchable by	Symbolic Type and Permissions	Octal Permissions
/var/spool/cron	owner (root)	owner (root)	owner (root) group (root) one everyone	-drwx-	700
/dev/tty1	owner (root)	owner (root) and group (tty)	owner (root)	crw--w---	625
/bin/chmod	owner (root) group (root) and everyone else	owner (root)	none	-rwxr-xr-x	755
/usr/bin/procmail	owner (root) group (mail), and everyone else	owner (root)	owner (root) group (mail) and everyone	-rwxr-xr-x	755
/usr/bin/locate	owner (root)	owner (root)	owner (root) group (root) permission every	-rwxr-s-x	274
/usr/bin/crontab	owner (root) group (root), and everyone else	owner (root)	owner (root) group (root) everyone with privilages	-rwsr-sr-x	6555

2. Change permissions.

   a. Make the Unit2/reports/report.feb file readable by the owner and group, writable by the owner only, and not available to others. *chmod 640 Unit2/reports/report.feb*

   b. Create a directory in /tmp named **shared**. The file should be owned by **mark** and associated with the group named **linux**. The user named **mark** and members of **linux** should have read, write, and execute permission. Other users should have no access. (Tip: Run these commands as the user **mark**.)
   mkdir /tmp/shared   *chmod 770 /tmp/shared*
   chgrp linux /tmp/shared

   c. Working as the user named **max**, create a file named max1 in the /tmp/shared directory. Attempt to create a file in /tmp/shared as while working as the user named **student**. Permission should be denied.

3. The permissions of a new file are determined by the file permissions mask that is set by the **umask** utility (Sobell, page 473).

   a. Working as the ordinary user named **student,** display the value of the file permissions mask.
   umask

   b. Create a new file named **mask.one** and view the permissions.
   touch mask.one   *ls -l mask.one*

   c. Change the file permissions mask to 077 and then create a file named **umask.two** and view the permissions.
   umask 077
   touch mask.two   *ls -l mask.two*

   d. Create a new directory named **masks** and view the permissions.
   mkdir mask
   ls -ld mask

4. Optional: Repeat the above procedure for other file permissions masks such as 027, 022, and 777.

DELIVERABLES:

Files and directories in /tmp and in the Unit2 subdirectory with specific ownership and permissions.

CHAPTER 6, LAB 2—SOLUTIONS:

1. Determine the permissions of various files and directories on the system. Fill in the chart below:

Filename	Readable by	Writable by	Executable/searchable by	Symbolic Type and Permissions	Octal Permissions
/etc/passwd	owner (root), group (root), and everyone else	owner (root)	none	-rw-r--r--	644
/etc/shadow	none	none	none	----------	000
/etc/cups/cupsd.conf	owner (root) and group (lp)	owner (root)	none	-rw-r-----	640
/var/log/audit	owner (root)	owner (root)	none	-rw-------	600
/var/log/cups	owner (lp), group (sys), and everyone else	owner (lp)	owner (lp), group (sys), and everyone else	drwxr-xr-x	755
/etc/cups/ssl	owner (root)	owner (root)	owner (root)	drwx------	700
/var/spool/mail	owner (root), group (root), and everyone else	owner (root) and group (root)	owner (root), group (root), and everyone else	drwxrwxr-x	775
/var/spool/cron	owner (root)	owner (root)	owner (root)	drwx------	700
/dev/tty1	owner (root)	owner (root) and group (tty)	none	crw--w----	620
/bin/chmod	owner (root), group (root), and everyone else	owner (root)	owner (root), group (root), and everyone else	-rwxr-xr-x	755
/usr/bin/procmail	owner (root), group (mail), and everyone else	owner (root)	owner (root), group (mail), and everyone else	-rwxr-xr-x	755
/usr/bin/locate	owner (root)	owner (root)	owner (root), group (root), and everyone else (with root privileges)	-rwx--s--x	2711
/usr/bin/crontab	owner (root), group (root), and everyone else	owner (root)	owner (root), group (root), and everyone else (with root privileges)	-rwsr-sr-x	6755

2. Change permissions.

    a. Make the Unit2/reports/report.feb file readable by the owner and group, writable by the owner only, and not available to others.

    chmod 640 Unit2/reports/report.feb

    or

    chmod o-r,g-w Unit2/reports/report.feb

    b. Create a directory in /tmp named **shared**. The file should be owned by **mark** and associated with the group named **linux**. The user named **mark** and members of **linux** should have read, write, and execute permission. Other users should have no access. (Tip: Run these commands as the user **mark**.)

    mkdir /tmp/shared

    chgrp linux /tmp/shared

    chmod 770 /tmp/shared

    c. n/a

3. The permissions of a new file are determined by the file permissions mask that is set by the **umask** utility (Sobell, page 473).

    a. Working as the ordinary user named **student,** display the value of the file permissions mask.

    umask

    b. Create a new file named **mask.one** and view the permissions.

    touch mask.one

    ls -l mask.one

    c. Change the file permissions mask to 077 and then create a file named **umask.two** and view the permissions.

    umask 077

    touch mask.two

    ls -l mask.two

    d. Create a new directory named **masks** and view the permissions.

    mkdir masks

    ls -ld masks

4. n/a

CHAPTER 6, LAB 3: SYSTEM ADMINISTRATION UTILITIES (30–40 MINUTES)

LEARNING OBJECTIVES AND OUTCOMES:

You should become more comfortable using the Linux command line by exploring commands used to monitor and manage a Linux system. Emphasis should be given to finding the commands and options on the system using the **man** and **info** utilities rather than memorizing every command and option from the text.

REQUIRED SETUP AND TOOLS:

- Fedora Linux 15 installation with an ordinary user (student) and the root password

ADDITIONAL RESOURCES:

- Sobell, Chapter 5

- man pages

- info pages

RECOMMENDED PROCEDURES:

1. Use the **grep** man page to help you form **grep** commands that accomplish the following tasks:

    a. Display each line in the /etc/passwd word that contains the string **student**.
        grep student /etc/passwd

    b. Verify that **mark** is a member of several groups by displaying all occurrences of **mark** in the /etc/group file.
        grep mark /etc/group

    c. List each occurrence of **student** in all the files in the /etc directory and its subdirectories.
        grep -R student /etc

    d. Instead of displaying each line in every file containing **student**, just list the filename of each file in the /etc directory that contains at least one line with **student**.
        grep -R -l student /etc

    e. Which lines in the /etc/group file reference **max**?
        grep -R max /etc   504 a

    f. List all the users in the /etc/passwd file who do *not* use the bash shell.
        grep -v bash /etc /password

    g. Display all references to the PATH variable (Sobell, page 308) in /etc/profile.
        grep PATH /etc/profile

h. The /etc/profile script modifies the PATH variable using a **pathmunge** command. List all references to both **PATH** and **pathmunge** with one query. (Tip: Look for uppercase and lowercase **path**.)

grep -i path /etc/profile

2. Use the man pages for **useradd**, **usermod**, **groupadd**, and **passwd** to form commands to complete the following tasks. (Tip: You will need to work with root privileges to perform these commands.)

   a. Create a group named **staff** with a gid of 1000.

   groupadd -g 1000

   b. Create a user named **jed** with a supplementary group of staff.

   useradd -G staff jed

   c. Add **mark** to the **staff** group.

   usermode -G staffmark

   d. Set the password for **jed** to **P@$$w0rd**.

   passwd jed

3. Viewing filesystem information and checking disk space from the command line.

   a. How much space is being used by Mark in his home directory?

   du-hs /home/mark   32 K

   b. How much space is being used by the /etc directory?

   du-hs /etc   30m

   c. How much free space is available in the root filesystem? Specify the answer in MB or GB.

   df -h   16 6

   d. Create a command that will display the percentage of free space in, and the filesystem type of, the filesystem mounted at /home.

   df -T /home   32%

4. Gather information about who is using the system.

   a. List the users currently logged in on the system.

   who   student tty1
               student pts6

   b. Determine when Mark last logged in on the system.

   last | grep mark | head

   c. Determine if there have been any failed logins. (Hint: You will need to work with root privileges.)

   lastb   6 21:20 - 21:20

5. View system information.

   a. Determine the amount of memory in the system.

   free -m   62

b. Display the current runlevel.

who -r *runlevel 5* 2

c. Determine how many CPUs are available.

grep processor /proc/cpuinfo | wc -l 1

DELIVERABLES:

Practice using system administration command-line utilities.

CHAPTER 6, LAB 3—SOLUTIONS:

1. Use the **grep** man page to help you form **grep** commands that accomplish the following tasks:

   a. Display each line in the /etc/passwd word that contains the string **student**.
      grep student /etc/passwd

   b. Verify that **mark** is a member of several groups by displaying all occurrences of **mark** in the /etc/group file.
      grep mark /etc/group

   c. List each occurrence of **student** in all the files in the /etc directory and its subdirectories.
      grep -R student /etc

   d. Instead of displaying each line in every file containing **student**, just list the filename of each file in the /etc directory that contains at least one line with **student**.
      grep -R -l student /etc

   e. Which lines in the /etc/group file reference **max**?
      grep -n max /etc/group

   f. List all the users in the /etc/passwd file who do *not* use the bash shell.
      grep -v bash /etc/passwd

   g. Display all references to the PATH variable. (Sobell, page 308) in /etc/profile.
      grep PATH /etc/profile

   h. The /etc/profile script modifies the PATH variable using a **pathmunge** command. List all references to both **PATH** and **pathmunge** with one query. (Tip: Look for uppercase or lowercase **path**.)
      grep -i path /etc/profile

2. Use the man pages for **useradd**, **usermod**, **groupadd**, and **passwd** to form commands to complete the following tasks. (Tip: You will need to work with root privileges to perform these commands.)

   a. Create a group named **staff** with a gid of 1000.
      groupadd -g 1000 staff

   b. Create a user named **jed** with a supplementary group of staff.
      useradd -G staff jed

   c. Add **mark** to the **staff** group.
      usermod -G staff mark

   d. Set the password for **jed** to **P@$$w0rd**.
      passwd jed

3. Viewing filesystem information and checking disk space from the command line.

   a. How much space is being used by Mark in his home directory? _____
      du -hs /home/mark

b. How much space is being used by the /etc/ directory? _____

du -hs /etc

c. How much free space is available in the root filesystem? Specify the answer in MB or GB. _____

df -h

d. Create a command that will display the percentage of free space in and the filesystem type of the filesystem mounted at /home.

df -T /home or **df -Th /home**

4. Gather information about who is using the system.

   a. List the users currently logged in on the system.

     Users or **who** or **w**

   b. Determine when Mark last logged in on the system.

     last | grep mark | head

   c. Determine if there have been any failed logins. (Hint: You will need to work with root privileges.)

     lastb

5. View system information.

   a. Determine the amount of memory in the system.

     free -m

   b. Display the current runlevel.

     who -r

   c. Determine how many CPUs are available.

     grep processor /proc/cpuinfo | wc -l

CHAPTER 6, LAB 4: WORKING WITH ACLS (15–20 MINUTES)

LEARNING OBJECTIVES AND OUTCOMES:

Extend traditional Linux file permissions by using ACL (Access Control List) rules.

REQUIRED SETUP AND TOOLS:

- Fedora Linux 15 installation with several ordinary users (student, mark, max, and jed). (Note: The users named **mark** and **max** were created in Chapter 4, Lab 1 and **jed** was created in Chapter 6, Lab 3; create these users if they do not exist. The group named **staff** was created, and **jed** and **mark** were added to this group, in Chapter 6, Lab 3; create this group and add **jed** and **mark** to it if necessary.)

ADDITIONAL RESOURCES:

- Sobell, Chapter 6, ACLs, pages 208–212

RECOMMENDED PROCEDURES:

1. Working as the user named **student**, create a directory in /tmp named **campaign**.

2. Display the standard access permissions for **campaign**.

3. Display the ACL permissions using **getfacl** (Sobell, page 209).

4. Adjust the permissions such that in addition to **student**'s current access

   a. Members of the group **staff** can read and access the directory (Sobell, page 203). The user **mark** should be a member of the group **staff**.

   b. The user named **jed** can read, write, and access the directory (Sobell, page 210).

   c. The user named **max** can only read and access the directory.

   d. Other users have no access to the directory. Create a new user named **bruno** to use while testing.

5. Test your permissions by working as each user and trying to view the contents of the directory and create a file in the directory.

6. Look at the permissions of the new files that **student** and **jed** created. Can **max** read the files? Write files to the directory?

7. Modify the ACLs so all new files created in the directory automatically allow **jed** to read and write files in the directory and **max** to read files in the directory.

8. Test the new permissions by creating a file in the directory and viewing the ACL rules.

DELIVERABLES:

A shared directory with access controlled by ACL rules.

CHAPTER 6, LAB 4—SOLUTIONS:

1. Working as the user named **student**, create a directory in /tmp named **campaign**.
   mkdir /tmp/campaign

2. Display the standard access permissions for campaign.
   ls -ld /tmp/campaign

3. Display the ACL permissions using **getfacl** (Sobell, page 209).
   getfacl /tmp/campaign

4. Adjust the permissions such that in addition to **student**'s current access

   a. Members of the group **staff** can read and access the directory (Sobell, page 203). The user **mark** should be a member of the group **staff**.
   chgrp linux /tmp/campaign
   chmod 750 /tmp/campaign
   Use the command id mark to check the group membership for the user mark and if necessary, add mark to the group staff by working with root privileges and giving the command usermod -a -G staff mark.

   b. The user named **jed** can read, write, and access the directory (Sobell, page 210).
   setfacl -m u:jed:rwx /tmp/campaign

   c. The user named **max** can only read and access the directory.
   setfacl -m u:max:rx /tmp/campaign

   d. Other users have no access to the directory. Create a new user named **bruno** to use while testing.
   chmod o-rwx /tmp/campaign
   useradd bruno
   passwd bruno

5. n/a

6. Look at the permissions of the new files that **student** and **jed** created. Can **max** read the files? Write files to the directory?
   getfacl filename
   Assuming the default umask of 002, max should be able to read the files created by other users but not write to those files; max cannot create files in the directory.

7. Modify the ACLs so all new files created in the directory automatically allow **jed** to read and write files in the directory and **max** to read files in the directory.
   setfacl -m d:u:jed:rw /tmp/campaign
   setfacl -m d:u:max:r /tmp/campaign

8. n/a

Chapter 7, Lab 1: Exploring bash Shell Special Characters (15–20 minutes)

Learning Objectives and Outcomes:

You will explore bash shell syntax for filename generation, output redirection, and variables.

Required Setup and Tools:

- Fedora Linux 15 installation with an ordinary user (student) and the root password

Additional Resources:

- Sobell, Chapter 9, page 346, brace expansion

- Sobell, Chapter 7, page 244, filename generation

- Sobell, Chapter 7, page 234, redirection

- Sobell, Chapter 7, page 239, pipes

Recommended Procedures:

Part I: Filename Generation Characters

1. Use brace expansion to create files for this exercise. Carefully type in the following command to create 36 files in your home directory.

   touch {report,memo,reminder}_{1,2,3,4}.{new,old,keep}

2. Create a directory named **Unit3** with subdirectories named **reports, memos, backups,** and **keepsakes.**

   mkdir -p unit3/reports unit3/memos unit3/Backup,

3. Organize your new files as follows. *unit3/keepsakes*

   a. Copy all files with names that end in **keep** to the keepsakes directory.

   b. Move all report files to the reports directory.

   unit3/reports

   c. Move all memo files to the memos directory.

   unit3/memos

   d. Remove all versions of reminders 1 and 2.

   unit3/ backup

   e. Copy the fourth version of the old files to the backups directory.

   unit3/keepsakes

4. Display the names of all the files in the Unit3 directory tree.

   ls -R unit3/

Part II: File Redirection and Pipes

5. Create a file named **ls.out** that contains a list of all files in the Unit3 directory hierarchy.

   ls -R Unit3 ls.out

6. Append the current time and today's date to the end of the **ls.out** file.

   date >> ls.out

7. Recreate the **grep** commands from Chapter 6, Lab 3 that search an entire directory of files. This time, redirect any permission denied errors to the null device.

   a. List each occurrence of **student** in the files in the /etc directory and its subdirectories.

   grep -R student /etc 2> /dev/null

   b. Instead of listing each line in each file that contains **student**, just list the filename of each file in the /etc directory that contains at least one line with **student**.

   grep -R -l student /etc/dev/nul

8. The **locate chess** command from Chapter 6, Lab 1 scrolled off the screen. Run the command again and view the output one screen at a time.

   locate chess | less

9. List all files with **chess** in their names that are *not* help files. (Hint: Use a pipe and **grep**.)

   locate chess | grep -v help

DELIVERABLES:

Organized files with the directory hierarchy recorded in the file ls.out.

Chapter 7, Lab 1—Solutions:

1. Use brace expansion to create files for this exercise. Carefully type in the following command to create 36 files in your home directory.

   touch {report,memo,reminder}_{1,2,3,4}.{new,old,keep}

2. Create a directory named **Unit3** with subdirectories named **reports, memos, backups**, and **keepsakes**.

   mkdir -p Unit3/reports Unit3/memos Unit3/backups Unit3/keepsakes

3. Organize your new files as follows.

   a. Copy all the files that end in **keep** to the keepsakes directory.

   cp *keep Unit3/keepsakes

   b. Move all the reports to the reports directory.

   mv report* Unit3/reports

   c. Move all the memo files to the memos directory.

   mv memo* Unit3/memos

   d. Remove all versions of reminders 1 and 2.

   rm reminder_[12]*

   e. Copy the fourth version of the old files to the backups directory.

   cp Unit3/*/*4.old Unit3/backups

4. View all the files in the Unit3 directory tree.

   ls -R Unit3/

5. Create a file named **ls.out** that contains a list of all the files in the Unit3 directory tree.

   ls -R Unit3 > ls.out

6. Append the date to the end of the **ls.out** file.

   date >> ls.out

7. Recreate the **grep** commands from Chapter 6, Lab 3 that search an entire directory of files. This time, redirect any permission denied errors to the null device.

   a. List each occurrence of student in all the files in the /etc directory and its subdirectories.

   grep -R student /etc 2>/dev/null

   b. Instead of listing each line in each file that contains **student**, just list the filename of any file in the /etc directory which contains at least one line with **student**.

   grep -R -l student /etc 2>/dev/null

8. The **locate chess** command from Chapter 6, Lab 1 scrolled off the screen. Run the command again and view the output one screen at a time.

   locate chess | less

9. List all files with **chess** in their name that are *not* help files (Hint: Use a pipe and **grep**.)

   locate chess | grep -v help

Chapter 9, Lab 1: Exploring More bash Shell Special Characters (15–20 minutes)

Learning Objectives and Outcomes:
You will explore bash shell syntax for variables and aliases.

Required Setup and Tools:

- Fedora Linux 15 installation with an ordinary user (student) and the root password

Additional Resources:

- Sobell, Chapter 9, page 307, keyword variables

- Sobell, Chapter 9, page 310, user prompt

- Sobell, Chapter 9, page 334, aliases

Recommended Procedures:
Viewing and Creating Variables and Aliases

1. Fill in the chart below:

Variable	As student	After gaining root privileges using su (no dash!)	After gaining root privileges using su -
HOSTNAME	student.example.com	student.example.com	student.example.com
PATH	/user/local/bin:/user/bin:/bin:/user/local/sbin:/user/sbin	/user/local/bin:/user/bin:/user/local/sbin:/user/sbin:/student	/user/local/bin:/user/bin:/root/bin:/user/local/sbin:/user/sbin
MAIL	/var/spool/mail/student	/var/spool/mail/student	/var/spool/mail/student
PWD	/home/student	/home/student	/root
USER	student	student	root

2. Append **/tmp/shared/bin** to your PATH variable. (Hint: You can use a variable while defining a variable.)

   PATH=$PATH:/tmp/shared/bin

3. Modify your shell prompt to include the current date at the beginning and the history number after the working directory. (Hint: Give the command **man bash** and search for **PROMPTING**.)

   PS1='\d[\u@\h \W]\!\$

4. Create an alias such that when the user types **lt Unit3**, the command displays a long, recursive listing of all files in the directory.

alias lt= 'ls -alR'

DELIVERABLES:

A customized bash shell environment.

CHAPTER 9, LAB 1—SOLUTIONS:

Viewing and Creating Variables and Aliases

1. Fill in the chart below:

Variable	As student	After gaining root privileges using su (no dash!)	After gaining root privileges using su -
HOSTNAME	linux.example.com	linux.example.com	linux.example.com
PATH	/usr/local/bin:/usr/bin:/bin: /usr/local/sbin:/usr/sbin:/sbin: /home/student/bin	/usr/local/bin:/usr/bin:/bin: /usr/local/sbin:/usr/sbin:/sbin: /home/students/bin	/usr/local/sbin:/usr/local/bin: /sbin:/bin:/usr/sbin:/usr/bin: /root/bin
MAIL	/var/spool/mail/student	/var/spool/mail/student	/var/spool/mail/root
PWD	/home/student	/home/student	/root
USER	student	student	root

Use the commands:

echo $HOSTNAME

echo $PATH

echo $MAIL

echo $PWD

echo $USER

2. Append **/tmp/shared/bin** to your PATH variable. (Hint: You can use a variable while defining a variable.)
    PATH=$PATH:/tmp/shared/bin

3. Modify your prompt to include the current date at the beginning and the history number after the working directory. (Hint: Give the command **man bash** and search for **PROMPTING**.)
    PS1='[\d][\u@\h \W]\! \$ '

4. Create an alias such that when the user types **lt Unit3**, the command displays a long, recursive listing of all files in the directory.
    alias lt='ls -alR'

CHAPTER 9, LAB 2: CUSTOMIZING USERS AND THE SYSTEM USING SCRIPTS (60–90 MINUTES)

LEARNING OBJECTIVES AND OUTCOMES:

You will modify and create scripts to manage the user environment and automate system administration tasks.

REQUIRED SETUP AND TOOLS:

- Fedora Linux 15 installation with an ordinary user (student or jed) and the root password

ADDITIONAL RESOURCES:

- Sobell, Chapter 9, page 288, shell scripts

- Sobell, Chapter 16, page 604, managing user accounts

RECOMMENDED PROCEDURES:

1. You have been asked to help Jed customize his shell environment. Preserve variable and alias definitions in the .bashrc and .bash_profile startup files.

    a. Members of the **staff** group will have a shared directory /staff/bin that holds scripts. Ensure that this directory is a part of Jed's PATH each time he logs in on the system.

        echo' PATH=$PATH: /staff/bin' >>/home/jed/.bash-Profile

    b. Jed has a habit of removing files with overly broad filename generation wildcards. Add an alias so that by default he is prompted to confirm each file he attempts to remove.

        /home/jed/.bashrc file alias rm='rm-i'

2. Write a script that generates a system activity report that includes disk and memory usage.

    a. Create a file.
    vim report.sh

    b. Begin the script with the magic **#!** (Sobell, page 290) and a comment to describe the purpose of the script.
    #!/bin/bash
    # This script will generate a report of system activity.

    c. Start the report with a date stamp.
    date

    d. Be sure the report indicates the hostname of the system.
    hostname

    e. Report on the amount of free disk space on the system.
    df -h

f.   Report on the amount of memory usage on the system.

free -m

g.   Determine if root is logged onto the system, and if so, report on which terminal root is using.

w | grep root

h.   You may want to clean up the output with some blank lines or descriptions.

i.   Save your script. It may look something like:

#!/bin/bash

 # This script will generate a report of system activity.

date

hostname

echo ""

df -h

echo ""

echo "root is logged on the following terminals"

w | grep root

j.   Place the new script in a directory that is in your PATH variable.

mkdir ~/bin

mv report.sh ~/bin

k.   Ensure that the new script is executable.

chmod 755 ~/bin/report.sh

l.   Test your script.

report.sh

3.   Write a script that will create the following users and groups:

Username	Group Membership
cjcraig	staff (1000) and press (1001)
toby	staff (1000) and press (1001) political (1002)
joshua	staff (1000) and political (1002)

All users should have the password **password**.

Use the man pages for **groupadd, useradd, usermod,** and **passwd** to form your commands.

Some of the commands you will likely use include:

groupadd -g 1000 staff

useradd -G staff,press cjcraig

echo password | passwd --stdin cjcraig

4. Create a script that will prompt the user through adding a user with specific group membership. Test your script by creating a user named **sam** who is a member of the **political** and **staff** groups, and then use the **id** utility to verify the account exists with the correct group membership.

    a. What happens when you try to create a user that already exists? (Try **max**.)
    You will be prompted for the group membership menu username
    should fail

    b. What happens if you try to create a user as a member of a group that does not exist? (Create **ansley** in the groups **staff** and **legal**.)
    The useradd command will fail with message command fail

5. Optional (using Sobell, Chapter 27): Add some conditional execution to your script that will create a group if it does not exist and will warn if the user already exists.

DELIVERABLES:

Customized login scripts for the user **jed**; a script that generates a report named **/tmp/report-date**, including disk space and memory usage; a script that creates a specific set of users and groups; and a script that prompts for a username and group membership and then creates that user.

CHAPTER 9, LAB 2—SOLUTIONS:

1. You have been asked to help Jed customize his shell environment. Preserve variable and alias definitions in the .bashrc and .bash_profile startup files.

   a. Members of the **staff** group will have a shared directory /staff/bin that holds scripts. Ensure that this directory is a part of Jed's PATH each time he logs in on the system.
   Use a text editor to edit the /home/jed/.bash_profile file or type the following command
   echo 'PATH=$PATH:/staff/bin' >> /home/jed/.bash_profile

   b. Jed has a habit of removing files with overly broad filename generation wildcards. Add an alias so that by default he is prompted to confirm each file he attempts to remove.
   Use an editor to add the following line to the /home/jed/.bashrc file
   alias rm='rm -i'

2. n/a

3. Write a script that will create the following users and groups:

```
#!/bin/bash
# A script to create a specific set of users that can be used on several machines
echo "creating group staff"
groupadd -i 1000 staff
echo "creating group press"
groupadd -i 1001 press
echo "creating group political"
groupadd -i 1002 political

echo "creating user cjcraig"
useradd -G staff,press cjcraig
echo password | passwd --stdin cjcraig
echo "the password for cjcraig is password"

echo "creating user toby"
useradd -G staff,political,press toby
echo password | passwd --stdin toby
echo "the password for toby is password"

echo "creating user joshua"
useradd -G staff,press joshua
echo password | passwd --stdin joshua
echo "the password for joshua is password"
```

4. Create a script that will prompt the user through adding a user with specific group membership.

   #!/bin/bash

   read -p "What username would you like? " USERNAME
   read -p "What group membership should be included for this user? " GROUPS
   useradd -G $GROUPS $USERNAME

   Test your script by creating a user named **sam** who is a member of the **political** and **staff** groups, and then use the **id** utility to verify the account exists with the correct group membership.

   a. What happens when you try to create a user that already exists? (Try **max**.)
      You will be prompted for the group membership, then the useradd command will fail with a user already exist message.

   b. What happens if you try to create a user as a member of a group that does not exist? (Create **ansley** in the group **staff** and **legal**.)
      The useradd command will fail with message that the group does not exist.

5. Optional (using Sobell, Chapter 27): Add some conditional execution to your script that will create a group if it does not exist and will warn if the user already exists.

   #!/bin/bash

   read -p "What username would you like? " USERNAME
   read -p "What group membership should be included for this user? " GROUPS

   for groupname in $GROUPS
   do
   grep -q $groupname /etc/group || groupadd $groupname
   done

   if $(grep -q $USERNAME /etc/passwd)
   then
    echo $USERNAME already exists, exiting
    exit 1
   else
    echo adding user $USERNAME
    useradd -G $GROUPS $USERNAME
   fi

Chapter 11, Lab 1: Exploring Runlevels (20–30 minutes)

Learning Objectives and Outcomes:

You should be able to determine the current runlevel, change between runlevels, and use virtual consoles.

Required Setup and Tools:

- Fedora Linux 15 installation with an ordinary user (student) and the root password

Additional Resources:

- Sobell, Chapter 4, page 138, virtual consoles

- Sobell, Chapter 11, page 448, runlevels

Recommended Procedures:

As a multiuser operating system, Fedora 15 allows multiple local logins using virtual consoles. You can switch between virtual consoles using the ALT key and function keys F1 through F6. F1 displays the graphical environment (if running) and F2–F6 display text-based logins. If you are in the graphical environment, you must also press the CONTROL key with the ALT-F[2-6] keys to switch to a different virtual console.

To change from the graphical desktop to the text-based virtual consoles while using VMware Player, you must also press the SHIFT key. Only include the SHIFT key when working in Vmware Player.

1. Using virtual consoles in Fedora

   a. Change to the text-based login on virtual console 2 by pressing SHIFT-CONTROL-ALT-F2. (Tip: Hold the SHIFT key before pressing the CONTROL-ALT combination or VMware Player will return control to the host desktop.)

   b. From the text console, log in as **student** and type **who** to see all users logged in on the system. Type **exit** or press CONTROL-D to log off.

   c. Return to the graphical desktop by pressing ALT-F1 or SHIFT-CONTROL-ALT-F1.

2. Switching runlevels

   a. Display a command prompt in a terminal emulator by selecting ApplicationsàSystem ToolsàTerminal. Start working with root privileges by typing **su –** and then entering the root password (Sobell, Chapter 11, page 413).

   b. Type **who -r** to display the current runlevel.

   c. Type **telinit 3** to change to runlevel 3.
      What happened to the graphical environment?

      Failed

d. Log in as root and type **who -r** to display the current runlevel.

e. Are other virtual consoles available?

Yes   change   with Alt -F3

f. Use **ping** to verify network connectivity (Sobell, Chapter 10, page 386).

ping -c3 192.68.100.83

g. Restart the graphical environment by entering **telinit 5**. Why did the system display the login prompt instead of the desktop?

when changing to runlevel 5 will true of graphical applications

h. Optional: Switch to runlevel 3 again, but this time, instead of using **telinit** to return to the graphical environment, reboot the system by typing **reboot**. Did the system boot to the graphical login? Why?

yes because I told it to reboot

3. Optional: Switch to runlevel 3 again, but this time, instead of using **telinit** to return to the graphical environment, reboot the system by typing **reboot**. Did the system boot to the graphical login? Why?

DELIVERABLES:

The ability to access virtual consoles and change runlevels.

Chapter 11, Lab 1—SOLUTIONS:

1. n/a

2. Switching runlevels

   a. n/a

   b. n/a

   c. Type **telinit 3** to change to runlevel 3.

   What happened to the graphical environment?

   The Graphical User Interface (GUI) application terminates when changing from runlevel 5 to runlevel 3.

   d. n/a

   e. Are other virtual consoles available?

   Yes. Change with ALT-F3, for example.

   f. Use ping to verify network connectivity (Sobell, page 386).

   ping -c3 *IP* where *IP* is the IP address of a remote system such as your the router

   g. Restart the graphical environment by entering **telinit 5**.

   Why did the system display the login prompt instead of the desktop?

   When changing to runlevel 3, all the graphical applications were terminated and all work in progress was lost. When returning to runlevel 5, scripts restart the graphical applications, resulting in a new login prompt and a new session.

3. Optional: Switch to runlevel 3 again, but this time, instead of using **telinit** to return to the graphical environment, reboot the system by typing **reboot**. Did the system boot to the graphical login. Why? **The telinit utility causes a temporary change to the current system state. When the system boots, it uses configuration files to determine the default runlevel. For more information see Sobell, page 432, "Setting the Persistent Runlevel."**

Chapter 11, Lab 2: Managing Network Services (15–20 minutes)

Learning Objectives and Outcomes:

You will initiate minimal network security by turning off unused services and verifying the status of the firewall.

Required Setup and Tools:

- Fedora Linux 15 installation with an ordinary user (student) and the root password

Additional Resources:

- Sobell, Chapter 11, pages 459–463, SELinux

- Sobell, Chapter 25, pages 893–895, Building a Firewall JumpStart

Introduction:

The most effective method of applying network security is to be disconnected from the Internet. A more practical procedure is to ensure that services not being used are not started at boot time. Beginning with Fedora 15, systemd manages most of the services and systemctl communicates your instructions to these services.

Recommended Procedures:

Part I: Try these commands to explore **systemctl**

1. **systemctl status NetworkManager.service**

2. **systemctl status network.service**

3. **systemctl is-enabled network.service**

4. **systemctl status sshd.service**

5. **systemctl enable sshd.service**

6. **systemclt stop ntpd.service**

7. **systemctl disable ntpd.service**

Part II: Exploring SELinux

SELinux is a MAC (Mandatory Access Control) security mechanism that can handle role-based access control, multi-level security, type enforcement, and other MAC methods. Fedora and Red Hat Enterprise Linux default installations enable SELinux in Enforcing mode and apply a policy that uses type enforcement. This setup can protect your system from damage when an intruder gains access to the system; however, it can also get in the way of adding additional software to the system until you have a stronger understanding of the contexts, Booleans, and policy involved in configuring SELinux.

View the SELinux configuration

8. Issue the command **sestatus**.

9. What is the current mode for SELinux?

   enforcing

10. What is the system default mode from the config file?

    enforcing

11. The configuration file mentioned in the output of sestatus is /etc/selinux/config. Working with root privileges, edit the /etc/selinux/config file and change the system default mode to **permissive**.

12. Does the **sestatus** utility show the new setting from the config file?

    Yes, the mode from the config file now show permission but the current mode is still enforced

13. Change the current mode using the command **setenforce permissive**.

Part III: View the current firewall configuration

14. Open the Firewall Configuration window by selecting ApplicationsàOtheràFirewall or, from the command line, give the command **system-config-firewall**. Enter the root password when prompted.

15. What are the currently trusted services?

    ssh and possibly the printing class

16. Disable the firewall now for use in the next unit. It will be enabled again later in the labs.

DELIVERABLES:

A disabled firewall that will be enabled in future labs.

Chapter 11, Lab 2—SOLUTIONS:

1.–7. n/a

8. Issue the command **sestatus**.

9. What is the current mode for SELinux?

   enforcing

10. What is the system default mode from the config file?

    enforcing

11. The configuration file mentioned in the output of sestatus is /etc/selinux/config. Working with root privileges, edit the /etc/selinux/config file and change the system default mode to **permissive**.

12. Does the **sestatus** utility show the new setting from the config file?

    Yes, the mode from the config file now shows permissive but the current mode is still enforcing.

13. Change the current mode using the command **setenforce permissive**.

14. What are the currently trusted services?

    ssh and possibly the printing client

15. n/a

16. n/a

CHAPTER 11, LAB 3: CONFIGURING DHCP SERVICES (25–35 MINUTES)

LEARNING OBJECTIVES AND OUTCOMES:

You will explore DHCP services before configuring them.

REQUIRED SETUP AND TOOLS:

- Fedora Linux 15 installation with an ordinary user (student) and the root password

- Access to the Fedora installation DVD or DVD ISO image file, used to install required client packages

- Internet access to the Fedora repository to install required server packages

ADDITIONAL RESOURCES:

- Sobell, Chapter 11, pages 489–493, DHCP

RECOMMENDED PROCEDURES:

Explore DHCP configuration.

1. If your system is a DHCP client, list the contents of the /var/lib/dhclient directory. View the dhclient-eth0.leases file (or any other leases file).

   a. Which nameserver was provided?

   b. Which router was provided?

   c. Which server provided the information?

   d. What is the renewal time?

   e. When does the lease expire?

2. If you have Internet connectivity, enable the Fedora repository and install the DHCP package.

3. *DO NOT START THE DHCP SERVER!* DHCP is a broadcast protocol. If there are multiple DHCP servers on a physical network, it is impossible to predict which server will answer a client request. Misconfigured systems and address collisions will result.

4. View the sample configuration file provided with the DHCP package.

   a. Which nameserver is offered for the 10.5.5.0 network?

   b. What is the maximum lease time for clients?

   c. Which range of addresses is offered to members of the foo class?

5. Create a new configuration file with the following specifications:

   a. Offer addresses from 172.20.0.50/24 through 172.20.0.254/24

   b. Place the router at 172.20.0.1

   c. Place the DNS server at 172.20.0.10

   d. Name the domain example.com

   e. Give the fixed address 172.20.0.5 and the name whitehouse.example.com to the system with the Ethernet hardware (MAC) address of 0:0:c0:5d:bd:95

6. Check the syntax of your configuration using one of the following commands:

   service dhcpd configtest

   dhcpd -t -cf /etc/dhcp/dhcpd.conf

DELIVERABLES:

A configuration file that can be used for a DHCP server.

CHAPTER 11, LAB 3—SOLUTIONS:

1. If your system is a DHCP client, list the contents of the /var/lib/dhclient directory. View the dhclient-eth0.leases file (or any other leases file).

   a. Which nameserver was provided?

      Varies; for example, option domain-name-servers 192.168.2.1

   b. Which router was provided?

      Varies; for example, option routers 192.168.5.1

   c. Which server provided the information?

      Varies; for example, option dhcp-server-identifier 192.168.5.1

   d. What is the renewal time?

      Varies; for example, 2011/07/11 12:06:35

   e. When does the lease expire?

      Varies; for example, 2011/07/12 02:31:36

2. If you have Internet connectivity, enable the Fedora repository and install the DHCP package.

   su -c 'yum --enablerepo=fedora install dhcp'

3. n/a

4. View the sample configuration file provided with the DHCP package.

   cat /etc/dhcp/dhcpd.conf

   less /usr/share/doc/dhcp-4*/dhcpd.conf.sample

   e. Which nameserver is offered for the 10.5.5.0 network?

      ns1.internal.example.org

   f. What is the maximum lease time for clients?

      7200 seconds = 2 hours

   g. Which range of addresses is offered to members of the foo class?

      10.17.224.10 – 10.17.224.250

5. Create a new configuration file with the following specifications:

a.–d. n/a

e. Give the fixed address 172.20.0.5 and the name whitehouse.example.com to the system with the Ethernet hardware (MAC) address of 0:0:c0:5d:bd:95

default-lease-time 600;

max-lease-time 7200;

ddns-update-style none;

subnet 172.20.0.0 netmask 255.255.255.0 {

> **range 172.20.0.50 172.20.0.254;**

> **option domain-name-servers 172.20.0.10;**

> **option domain-name "example.com";**

> **option routers 172.20.0.1;**

> **}**

host whitehouse {

> **hardware ethernet 0:0:c0:5d:bd:95;**

> **fixed-address 172.20.0.5;**

> **}**

6. n/a

CHAPTER 11, LAB 4: GAINING ROOT PRIVILEGES USING SUDO (15–20 MINUTES)

LEARNING OBJECTIVES AND OUTCOMES:

Configure sudo to allow select users to issue some administration commands using root privileges without needing to know the root password.

REQUIRED SETUP AND TOOLS:

- Fedora Linux 15 installation with an ordinary user (student) and the root password (Note: The users named **mark** and **max** were created in Chapter 4, Lab 1; **jed** was created in Chapter 6, Lab 3; create these users if they do not exist.)

ADDITIONAL RESOURCES:

- Sobell, Chapter 11, pages 415–425, sudo

RECOMMENDED PROCEDURES:

1. Working with root privileges, use **visudo** to modify the /etc/sudoers file (Sobell, page 419). Add a line that grants the user named **student** full root privileges.

2. Working as **student**, view the /var/log/messages file without and then with sudo.

3. Working with root privileges, use **visudo** to modify the /etc/sudoers file. Add lines that

   a. Add a user alias named **ADMIN** that includes **max** and **jed**.

   b. Add a command alias named **MEDIA** that includes **mount** and **umount**.

   c. Allow **ADMIN** users and **jed** to run the **MEDIA** commands.

4. Working as **jed**, **mark**, or **max**, test sudo using following steps:

   a. Look for the /boot filesystem using **df -h** or **mount**.

   b. Attempt to unmount /boot without using **sudo**.

   c. Use **sudo** to unmount /boot.

   d. Verify the /boot filesystem is no longer available using **df -h** or **mount**.

e. Make /boot available using **mount /boot**.

f. Ensure the user **jed, max,** or **mark** cannot run other commands using **sudo**. For example, attempt to view the /var/log/messages file.

Deliverables:

A sudoers file granting the user **student** full administration privileges and granting select privileges to some other users.

CHAPTER 11, LAB 4—SOLUTIONS:

1. Working with root privileges, use **visudo** to modify the /etc/sudoers file (Sobell, page 419). Add a line that grants the user named **student** full root privileges.

   student ALL=(ALL)　　ALL

2. Working as **student**, view the /var/log/messages file without and then with sudo.

   tail /var/log/messages

   sudo tail /var/log/messages

3. Working with root privileges, use **visudo** to modify the /etc/sudoers file. Add lines that

   a. Add a user alias named **ADMIN** that includes **max** and **jed**.

      User_Alias ADMIN = max, jed

   b. Add a command alias named **MEDIA** that includes **mount** and **umount**.

      Cmnd_Alias　　　MEDIA = /bin/mount, /bin/umount

   c. Allow **ADMIN** users and **jed** to run the **MEDIA** commands.

      ADMIN, mark　　ALL=(ALL)　　MEDIA

4. Working as **jed**, **mark**, or **max**, test sudo using following steps:

   a. n/a

   b. Attempt to unmount /boot without using **sudo**.

      umount /boot

   c. Use **sudo** to unmount /boot.

      sudo umount /boot

   d. n/a

   e. Make /boot available using **mount /boot**.

      sudo mount /boot

   f. Ensure the user **jed**, **max**, or **mark** cannot run other commands using **sudo**. For example, attempt to view the /var/log/messages file.

      sudo less /var/log/messages

CHAPTER 13, LAB 1: INSTALLING SOFTWARE USING YUM (15–20 MINUTES)

LEARNING OBJECTIVES AND OUTCOMES:

You will list installed software packages and search available software packages using yum.

REQUIRED SETUP AND TOOLS:

- Fedora Linux 15 installation with an ordinary user (student) and the root password

- Access to the Fedora installation DVD or DVD ISO image file

ADDITIONAL RESOURCES:

- Sobell, Chapter 13

RECOMMENDED PROCEDURES:

1. To use **yum**, a collection of software packages called a *repository* must be made available and the local system must know where to look for these packages. At installation, Fedora 15 configures the system to look for available packages on the Internet at any Fedora mirror site. Many companies have systems behind firewalls and do not allow Internet access. We will use the Fedora installation DVD or ISO image file as our source of additional packages.

   a. Open a terminal emulator and gain root privileges.

   b. Disable the Internet mirrors by moving the configuration files to your home directory.

   c. Insert the Fedora installation DVD in your local system.

   d. Copy the **company internal** repository configuration file from classroom server to the /etc/yum.repos.d directory using the following command:
   scp mark@server:/var/ftp/pun/class.repo /etc/yum.repos.d
   Or create a file in the /etc/yum.repos.d directory named class.repo with the following content:
   [class-DVD]
   name=Class DVD repobaseurl=file:///media/Fedora\ 15\ i386\ DVD
   gpgcheck=0
   enabled=1

   e. Troubleshooting: If you have recently used **yum**, you may need to remove any cache by giving the command **yum clean all**.

f. Troubleshooting: If you cannot retrieve the repository, confirm that SELinux is in permissive mode by giving the command **setenfore permissive.**

g. Troubleshooting: Verify that the Fedora installation DVD is available at /media/Fedora\ 15\ i386\ DVD. If the DVD appears in a different location, modify the /etc/yum.repos.d/class.repo file accordingly.

2. Use **yum** to answer the following queries. You can find valid **yum** commands in the man page or in the text (Sobell, page 540).

a. Which version of bash is installed?

yum list bash bash.i

b. Which installed package names begin with the string **kernel**?

Yum list installed "Kernel"

c. Which system-config tools are available for installation?

yum list available system-config

d. Which groups of packages are installed and available?

yum group list

e. Which packages of the Printing client group are optional?

Yum groupinfo "Printing support

f. Which security scanner software is available?

Yum search scan, yum search security

g. Optional: Which package provides the Apache Web Services? (Hint: The Web protocol is HTTP.)

h. Optional: Which package provides the sshd_config file? Which package provides the vsftpd.conf file?

3. Practice installing and removing software (Sobell, JumpStart on page 534) by installing the **httpd** and **createrepo** packages and then removing the **httpd** and **python-deltarpm** packages.

4. Reinstall the **httpd** package. It will be used in an upcoming lab.

DELIVERABLES:

Confirm for your instructor that the **createrepo** and **httpd** packages are installed on your system.

CHAPTER 13, LAB 1—SOLUTIONS:

1. To use **yum**, a collection of software packages must be made available and the local system must know where to look for these packages. At installation, Fedora 15 configures the system to look for available packages on the Internet at any Fedora mirror site. Many companies have systems behind firewalls and do not allow Internet access. We will use the Fedora installation DVD or ISO image file as our source of additional packages.

   a. Open a terminal emulator and gain root privileges.

   Applicationsà System Toolsà Terminal

   su -

   b. Disable the Internet mirrors by moving the configuration files to your home directory.
   mv /etc/yum.repos.d/*repo ~

   c.–f. n/a

   c. Troubleshooting: Verify that the Fedora installation DVD is available at /media/Fedora\ 15\ i386\ DVD. If the DVD appears in a different location, modify the /etc/yum.repos.d/class.repo file accordingly.
   ls /media
   If the /media directory is empty, insert and allow GNOME to mount your DVD. If you are using VMWare or Virtual Box, you may need to disconnect the DVD and reconnect the DVD.
   If the /media directory has a different name for the directory containing files on the DVD, edit the /etc/yum.repos.d/class.repo file and change the path of the baseurl entry.

2. Use **yum** to answer the following queries. You can find valid **yum** commands in the man page or in the text (Sobell, page 540).

   a. Which version of bash is installed?
   yum list bash

   b. Which installed package names begin with the string **kernel**?
   yum list installed "kernel*"

   c. Which system-config tools are available for installation?
   yum list available system-config*

   d. Which groups of packages are installed and available?
   yum grouplist

   e. Which packages of the Printing client group are optional?
   yum groupinfo "Printing Support"

   f. Which security scanner software is available?
   yum search scanner
   yum search "security scanner"

g. Optional: Which package provides the Apache Web Services? (Hint: The Web protocol is HTTP.)

yum search httpd

h. Optional: Which package provides the sshd_config file? Which package provides the vsftpd.conf file?

yum whatprovides "*/sshd_config"

yum whatprovides "*/vsftpd.conf"

3. Practice installing and removing software (Sobell, JumpStart on page 534) by installing the **httpd** and **createrepo** packages and then removing the **httpd** and **python-deltarpm** packages.

yum install httpd

yum install createrepo

yum remove httpd

yum remove python-deltarpm

4. Reinstall the **httpd** package. It will be used in an upcoming lab.

yum install httpd

CHAPTER 13, LAB 2: INSTALLING SOFTWARE USING RPM (10–15 MINUTES)

LEARNING OBJECTIVES AND OUTCOMES:

You will install packages and dependencies using the rpm utility.

REQUIRED SETUP AND TOOLS:

- Fedora Linux 15 installation with an ordinary user (student) and the root password

- Access to the Fedora installation DVD or DVD ISO image file

ADDITIONAL RESOURCES:

- Sobell, Chapter 13, pages 547–551, RPM package manager

RECOMMENDED PROCEDURES:

The **yum** utility provides the advantage of searching multiple locations for software and also resolving dependencies. Continuing with the setup from the previous lab (Chapter 13, Lab 1), install the same packages as you did when you followed the instructions in the JumpStart section of the text (page 534), but this time use the **rpm** utility. The packages are in the /media/Fedora* directory.

1. Ensure that ypbind and yp-tools are not installed. Allow **yum** to also remove any other dependencies.

   yum remove yp-tools ybind

2. Install ypbind using the **rpm** utility and notice the dependency errors.

   rpm -ivh /media/fedora/packages/ypbind.rpm

3. Install both ypbind and yp-tools. Continue resolving dependencies until ypbind is installed.

4. Remove yp-tools using **rpm** and note the dependency errors.

5. Remove yp-tools and ypbind.

6. Install the **createrepo** package. Leave this package installed; it will be used in an upcoming lab.

DELIVERABLES:

Confirm that the **createrepo** and **httpd** packages are installed on your system.

CHAPTER 13, LAB 2—SOLUTIONS:

1. Ensure that ypbind and yp-tools are not installed. Allow **yum** to also remove any other dependencies.
   yum remove yp-tools ypbind

2. Install ypbind using the **rpm** utility and notice the dependency errors.
   rpm -ivh /media/Fedora*/Packages/ypbind-*.rpm

3. Install both ypbind and yp-tools. Continue resolving dependencies until ypbind is installed.
   rpm -ivh /media/Fedora*/Packages/rpcbind*rpm
   rpm -ivh /media/Fedora*/Packages/ypbind*rpm /media/Fedora*/Packages/yp-tools*.rpm

4. Remove yp-tools using **rpm** and note the dependency errors.
   rpm -e yp-tools

5. Remove yp-tools and ypbind.
   rpm -e yp-tools ypbind

6. Install the **createrepo** package. Leave this package installed; it will be used in an upcoming lab.
   rpm -ivh /media/Fedora*/Packages/createrepo*rpm /media/Fedora*/Packages/python-deltarpm*rpm

Chapter 13, Lab 3: Installing Software from Source Code Files (15–30 minutes)

Learning Objectives and Outcomes:
You will install software from source code files.

Required Setup and Tools:

- Fedora Linux 15 installation with an ordinary user and the root password

- Access to the Fedora installation DVD or DVD ISO image file

Additional Resources:

- Sobell, Chapter 13, page 552, GNU Configure and Build System

Recommended Procedures:

The **yum** and **rpm** utilities install software that has already been compiled. Sometimes an **rpm** package is not available for a program; other times you may want to compile the software yourself so that you can modify the configuration or add a patch.

Optional (requires Internet access or other access to a source tar file): Download the source code tar file for a package from gnu.org, such as the **which** package. Compile and install the package (Sobell, pages 552–553).

1. Verify that the Development Tools group was installed as instructed in Chapter 3, Lab 1.

2. Extract the files from the tar file and read any README or INSTALL files.

3. Configure the source code.

4. Compile the source code.

5. Install the program. Note where the program gets installed.

6. Test the program.

7. How would you remove the program?

8. How would you query the system to determine if the program is installed?

Deliverables:
Confirm that the **which** utility is installed on your system.

CHAPTER 13, LAB 3—SOLUTIONS:

Optional (requires Internet access or other access to a source tar file): Download the source code tar file for a package from gnu.org, such as the **which** package. Compile and install the package (Sobell, pages 552–553).

1. Verify that the Development Tools group was installed as instructed in Chapter 3, Lab 1.
    yum grouplist | grep Tools

2. Follow the steps in Chapter 13, pages 552–553.

3. Follow the steps in Chapter 13, pages 552–553.

4. Follow the steps in Chapter 13, pages 552–553.

5. Follow the steps in Chapter 13, pages 552–553.

6. Follow the steps in Chapter 13, pages 552–553.

7. How would you remove the program?
    Some source code comes with a uninstall script or an uninstall option to the make utility. In other cases, you will need to locate and remove each file manually.

8. How would you query the system to determine if the program is installed?
    You cannot easily remove or query the system for a program installed from source files. RPM makes queries a less tedious administration task

Chapter 13, Lab 4: Troubleshooting Using RPM Queries (20–30 minutes)

Learning Objectives and Outcomes:

You will investigate package contents before and after installation using **rpm** query and verify commands.

Required Setup and Tools:

- Fedora Linux 15 installation with an ordinary user (student) and the root password

- Access to the Fedora installation DVD or DVD ISO image file

Additional Resources:

- Sobell, Chapter 13

Recommended Procedures:

Some queries can be performed using either **yum** or **rpm**. Compare **yum** and **rpm** queries:

1. List installed packages.

2. List installed packages using wildcards.

3. List available packages.

4. Get information about an installed package.

5. Get information about a package that is not installed.

Some queries are considerably easier using **yum**.

6. Find out which package provides the **createrepo** utility

Some queries are only possible using **rpm**.

7. List the files that are a part of the **logrotate** and **wireshark-gnome** packages.

8. View the pre- and post-install scripts for the **httpd** package.

9. View the changelog of the **httpd** package.

DELIVERABLES:

None.

CHAPTER 13, LAB 4—SOLUTIONS:

1. List installed packages.

    yum list installed logrotate

    rpm -q logrotate

2. List installed packages using wildcards.

    yum list installed *kernel*

    rpm -qa | grep kernel

3. List available packages.

    yum list wireshark

    rpm -q wireshark (reports "package wirshark is not installed")

    ls /media/Fedora*/Packages/wireshark*

4. Get information about an installed package.

    yum info createrepo

    rpm -qi createrepo

5. Get information about a package that is not installed.

    yum info wireshark-gnome

    rpm -qip /media/Fedora*/Packages/wireshark-gnome*rpm

6. Find out which package provides the **createrepo** utility

    yum whatprovides "*createrepo"

    rpm -q --whatprovides createrepo

    rpm -qf /usr/bin/createrepo (only works with an installed package)

7. List the files that are a part of the **logrotate** and **wireshark-gnome** packages.

    rpm -ql logrotate

    rpm -qlp /media/Fedora*/Packages/wireshark-gnome*rpm

8. View the pre- and post-install scripts for the **httpd** package.

    rpm -q --scripts httpd

9. View the changelog of the **httpd** package.

    rpm -q --changelog httpd

CHAPTER 13, LAB 5: CREATING AND MANAGING YUM REPOSITORIES (20–30 MINUTES)

LEARNING OBJECTIVES AND OUTCOMES:

You will configure your systems to connect to additional **yum** repositories and you will make RPM source (RPMS) files available to other systems through a **yum** repository.

REQUIRED SETUP AND TOOLS:

- Fedora Linux 15 installation with an ordinary user (student) and the root password

- Access to the Fedora installation DVD or DVD ISO image file

- Optional: Access to the classroom server hosting an additional repository

ADDITIONAL RESOURCES:

- Sobell, Chapter 13

RECOMMENDED PROCEDURES:

1. Examine existing configuration files.

    a. /etc/yum.conf

    b. /etc/yum.repos.d/class.repo

    c. Return the repo files to their original location.

    d. Disable the Fedora default (Internet) repositories.

2. Assume demand for the additional kernel packages is high. You have been asked to host a copy of these packages as an additional repository. Clients expect to be able to install packages from http://linux.example.com/packages.

    a. Install the **httpd** package to provide a Web server and start the httpd daemon.

    b. Copy (mirror) all kernel files from the DVD to /var/www/html/packages.

    c. Use **createrepo** to establish the metadata for the new repository.

3. Optional: The additional packages are also on the classroom server and available at http://server/package. You should plan to periodically check the server for additional packages.

    a. Create a script that will run **rsync** then **createrepo.**

    b. Once your script works, place it in the /etc/cron.daily directory. (The **crond** daemon is covered in Sobell, page 611.)

4. Configure your system to use the local repository instead of the server repository.

5. Test with
yum clean all
yum list available kernel

DELIVERABLES:

A new repository of kernel RPMS files and modified class.repo file.

CHAPTER 13, LAB 5—SOLUTIONS:

1. Examine existing configuration files.

   a. n/a

   b. n/a

   c. Return the repo files to their original location.
      cp ~/*repo /etc/yum.repos.d

   d. Disable the Fedora default (Internet) repositories.
      Edit the files and change enabled=1 to enabled=0

2. Assume demand for the additional kernel packages is high. You have been asked to host a copy of these packages as an additional repository. Clients expect to be able to install packages from http://linux.example.com/packages.

   a. Install the **httpd** package to provide a Web server and start the httpd daemon.
      yum install httpd
      systemctl start httpd.service
      systemctl enable httpd.service

   b. Copy (mirror) all kerrnel files from the DVD to /var/www/html/packages.
      mkdir /var/www/html/packages
      rsync /media/Fedora*/Packages/kernel* /var/www/html/packages

   c. Use **createrepo** to establish the metadata for the new repository.
      createrepo -v /var/www/html/packages

3. Optional: The additional packages are also on the classroom server and available at http://server/package. You should plan to periodically check the server for additional packages.

   a. Create a script that will run **rsync** then **createrepo**.
      Create a file pkgupdates.sh with the following three lines:
      #!/bin/bash
      rsync /media/Fedora*/Packages/kernel* /var/www/html/packages
      createrepo -v /var/www/html/packages

      Make sure the script is exectuable:
      chmod +x pkgupdates.sh

      Working with root privilege, test your script:
      su -c 'pkgupdates.sh'

b. Once your script works, place it in the /etc/cron.daily directory. (The **crond** daemon is covered in Sobell, page 611.)

su -c 'cp pkgupdates.sh /etc/cron.daily'

su -c 'chmod +x /etc/cron.daily/plgupdates.sh'

4. Configure your system to use the local repository instead of the server repository.

Edit the /etc/yum.repo.d/class.repo file and change the baseurl to http://localhost/packages.

5. n/a

Chapter 14, Lab 1: Add a Local, Text-Only Printer (20–30 minutes)

Learning Objectives and Outcomes:

You will configure the system to print to a local printer.

Required Setup and Tools:

- Fedora Linux 15 installation with an ordinary user (student) and the root password

Additional Resources:

- Sobell, Chapter 14, page 565, JumpStart II

Recommended Procedures:

1. Display the Printing window.

   Select Applications⇒Other⇒ Printing or, from the command line give the command system - config-printer

2. Click **Add** to configure a new printer and enter the root password when prompted.

   a. If asked about configuring the firewall, click **Adjust Firewall**.

   b. Click **Serial Port #1**, leave the default settings, and click **Forward**.

   c. Because no printer is attached to the system, Fedora will not find any drivers. Use the Generic make from the printer database, and on the next screen, use the text-only driver.

   d. Name your printer *class-name* where *class* indicates your course and *name* is your name or initials. For example: nt1430-mark

   e. Optional: Specify a printer description.

   f. Do *not* send a test page.

3. Right-click the new printer icon and select Properties to view or modify settings.

4. Right-click the new printer icon and select Set as Default to make this printer the system default printer.

5. Use the command line to view your printer settings.

   lpstat -a
   lpq

6. Use the command line to print the /etc/hosts file to the default printer.

7. The output should "print" too quickly to view in the queue. Disable the queue and print the /etc/hosts file again.

8. Send a second job to the disabled print queue. This time, print the /etc/sysconfig/network file, and then delete the job. (Hint: You will need to look up the print job number.)

lpr /etc/sysconfig/network   lprm jobnumber
lpq

9. Re-enable the print queue, and then check that the remaining job was released.

lpw

su -c' cupsenable class-name'
lpq

DELIVERABLES:

A local default print queue.

CHAPTER 14, LAB 1—SOLUTIONS:

1. Display the Printing window.

   Select Applicationsà Otherà Printing or, from the command line, give the command

   system-config-printer

2.–4. n/a

5. Use the command line to view your printer settings.

   lpstat -a

   lpq

6. Use the command line to print the /etc/hosts file to the default printer.

   lpr /etc/hosts

7. The output should "print" too quickly to view in the queue. Disable the queue and print the /etc/hosts file again.

   cupsdisable class-name

   lpr /etc/hosts

   lpq

8. Send a second job to the disabled print queue. This time, print the /etc/sysconfig/network file, and then delete the job. (Hint: You will need to look up the print job number.)

   lpr /etc/sysconfig/network

   lpq

   lprm job number

   lpq

9. Re-enable the print queue, and then check that the remaining job was released.

   su -c ' cupsenable class-name'

   lpq

Chapter 14, Lab 2: Using CUPS to Connect to a Remote Printer (10–15 minutes)

Learning Objectives and Outcomes:

Define a local printer queue to print to a remote IPP printer.

Required Setup and Tools:

- Fedora Linux 15 installation with an ordinary user (student) and the root password

- Access to the classroom server that shares a printer using CUPS (Note: On the classroom server, the printer named foobar "prints" to a Web page. You can check the output of a print job using a browser to view the printed page at http://server.example.com/printers/foobar.)

Additional Resources:

- Sobell, Chapter 14

Recommended Procedures:

1. Select ApplicationsàOtheràPrinting or give the command **system-config-printer** to display the Printing window (Sobell, page 562).

2. In the Printing window, click **Add** to create a new printer.

3. After providing the root password, expand the Network Printer section and click **Find Network Printer**.

4. Search the classroom server (server.example.com) for available printers.

5. Verify the foobar printer. If foobar is not the default, look for it under Connection at the bottom of the screen.

6. On the next screens, choose the driver for the Generic printer manufacturer, text-only model.

7. Give your printer a local queue name of **remote-*name*** where ***name*** is your name or initials. Optionally, you can add a description.

8. Do *not* make this printer the default printer.

9. Test your printer by sending your /etc/hosts file from the command line. (The test page is not text and will not print.)

10. The output of the foobar printer can be viewed by pointing a Web browser (Firefox) at http://server.example.com/printers/foobar.

Deliverables:

A local printer queue for the remote printer foobar.

CHAPTER 14, LAB 2—SOLUTIONS:

1.–8. n/a

9. Test your printer by sending your /etc/hosts file from the command line. (The test page is not text and will not print.)

   lpr -P remote-*name* /etc/hosts

10. n/a

Chapter 15, Lab 1: Learning About GRUB (25–35 minutes)

Learning Objectives and Outcomes:

Use GRUB to manage the boot process and to pass boot parameters to the kernel.

Required Setup and Tools:

- Fedora Linux 15 installation with an ordinary user (student) and the root password

Additional Resources:

- Sobell, Chapter 3, page 67, Modifying Boot Parameters

- Sobell, Chapter 11, page 450, Boot the System to Single-User Mode

- Sobell, Chapter 15, page 595, GRUB

Recommended Procedures:

1. Preparation

    a. Edit the /boot/grub/grub.conf file and change **default=0** to **default=15**.

    b. Display the current runlevel.

    c. Display the default target (runlevel).

2. Use GRUB to boot to the multiuser target (runlevel 3).

    a. Reboot the system and hold the SHIFT key to interrupt the boot process and view the GRUB menu.

    b. Use the ARROW keys to select the default kernel.

    c. Press **a** to append an option to the kernel.

    d. Add the argument **3** to the kernel line to boot to the multiuser target (runlevel 3) and press ENTER.

3. Verify the results.

    a. Display the current runlevel

    b. Display the default target

    c. View the /boot/grub/grub.conf file

4. Reboot the system to verify that the change was temporary. The system should boot to a graphical login prompt.

5. If you have Internet access, enable the Fedora repository and install the kernel documentation package.

6. Using the /usr/share/doc/kernel-doc*/Documentation/kernel-parameters.txt file, determine a boot parameter to pass pass to the kernel using GRUB that will

   a. Force the system to boot with SELinux in permissive mode.

   b. Set the maximum number of processors for use to 4.

   c. Prompt for a video mode for the text-based terminals.

   d. Load the kernel and start the bash shell instead of the init process.

7. Modify your /boot/grub/grub.conf file so the system always boots with SELinux in permissive mode.

8. Reboot and use **getenforce** to verify the SELinux mode (Sobell, page 462). View the contents of /proc/cmdline to verify that the parameter was passed at boot time.

DELIVERABLES:

A modified GRUB configuration file.

CHAPTER 15, LAB 1—SOLUTIONS:

1. Preparation

   a. n/a

   b. Display the current runlevel.
      who -r

   c. Display the default target (runlevel).
      ls -l /etc/systemd/system/default.target
      (RHEL6: **grep initdefault /etc/inittab**)

2. n/a

3. Verify the results.

   a. Display the current runlevel.
      who -r

   b. Display the default target.
      ls -l /etc/systemd/system/default.target
      (RHEL6: **grep initdefault /etc/inittab**)

   c. View the /boot/grub/grub.conf file.
      less /boot/grub/grub.conf

4. n/a

5. If you have Internet access, enable the Fedora repository and install the kernel documentation package.
   yum --enablerepo=fedora install kernel-doc

6. Using the /usr/share/doc/kernel-doc*/Documentation/kernel-parameters.txt file, determine a boot parameter to pass pass to the kernel using GRUB that will

   a. Force the system to boot with SELinux in permissive mode.
      enforcing=0

   b. Set the maximum number of processors for use to 4.
      maxcpus=4

   c. Prompt for a video mode for the text-based terminals.
      vga=ask

   d. Load the kernel and start the bash shell instead of the init process.
      init=/bin/bash

9. n/a

10. Reboot and use **getenforce** to verify the SELinux mode (Sobell, page 462). View the contents of /proc/cmdline to verify that the parameter was passed at boot time.

getenforce

cat /proc/cmdline

CHAPTER 16, LAB 1: CONTROLLING PROCESSES (30–40 MINUTES)

LEARNING OBJECTIVES AND OUTCOMES:

Monitor, schedule, and send signals to processes.

REQUIRED SETUP AND TOOLS:

- Fedora Linux 15 installation with an ordinary user (student) and the root password

ADDITIONAL RESOURCES:

- Sobell, Chapter 16

RECOMMENDED PROCEDURES:

1. Launch the GNOME System Monitor by selecting ApplicationsàSystem ToolsàSystem Monitor. You might want to maximize the System Monitor window to make it easier to view.

    a. To view processes, click the **Processes** tab.

    b. Use the View menu on the menubar to switch between viewing My Processes and All Processes.

    c. Sort on a field by clicking the column title.

    d. Which process on the system is using the most CPU power (the highest percentage)? _____

    e. Which of My Processes is using the most memory? _____

    f. Add fields by clicking EditàPreferences and then placing a tick in the check box next to each of the Information Fields. Add the User and the (SELinux) Security Context to the display.

    g. Explore other options and tabs in the System Monitor window.

2. Processes can also be monitored in a textual environment using the **top** utility from a terminal window (Sobell, page 616).

    a. From the information at the top of the screen, how long has your system been running? _____

    b. To display the processes of the user named **student** only, press **u** then type **student** and press ENTER. To show all processes again, press **u** and then ENTER.

    c. To sort by a specific field press **F** and then press the letter for the field to sort on.

    d. Which process owned by **student** is using the most %CPU? _____

    e. Which process on the system is using the highest percentage of memory? _____

    f. Use **h** to display Help. Which key allows you to change the order of the fields?_____

    g. Add the parent process ID (PPID) field to your display.

h. Save the configuration so that **top** displays PPID every time you start it.

i. Use **q** to quit **top**.

3. Processes can be listed from the command line using the **ps** utility (Sobell, page 317).

 d. By default, **ps** displays the processes started from your current shell. What is the PID (process ID) of the current shell?_____

 e. View all processes using **ps -ef** or **ps aux**.

 f. To view processes owned by **student** use **ps -Ustudent**

 g. To find the processes running bash, list all processes and pipe through **grep**.

 h. You can customize the output using the -o option. List all processes with only the UID (user ID), PID (process ID), and command being run by the process using **ps -ouid,pid,comm**

 i. List the current shell processes including the PID, PPID, owner, and command.

4. A hung process might be terminated by sending it a signal using the **kill** utility (Sobell, page 470).

 a. Run the **sleep** utility in the background by giving the command **sleep 100 &**.

 b. Find the PID using **ps** and then terminate the process using **kill** with the default TERM signal.

 c. Open another terminal window and determine the process ID of the bash process running in the terminal window.

 d. Use **kill** to terminate this bash process. Try a TERM signal first. Did that work? Which signal will force the termination of the process?

5. Modify the report.sh script from Chapter 9 to also list all the bash processes running on the system. Set up the command to display the owner, PID, terminal (TTY), and command.

6. Working as **student,** use **crontab** to schedule report.sh to run every Mon/Wed/Fri at 8am (Sobell, User crontab files, page 612).

7. Have Max issue a command to back up his home directory.

 a. Use tar to create the file /tmp/max_home.tar.

 b. Modify the tar command to add gzip compression and name the file /tmp/max_home.tgz.

c. Modify the command so the output filename includes the current date using command substitution (Sobell, page 351). (Hint: The command **date +%Y%m%d** will provide a nicely formatted date.)

d. Schedule the job to run every Saturday at 10pm.

DELIVERABLES:

A modified report script including process monitoring scheduled to run on a regular schedule.

CHAPTER 16, LAB 1—SOLUTIONS:

1. n/a

2. n/a

3. Processes can be listed from the command line using the **ps** utility (Sobell, page 317).

    a.–c. n/a

    d. To find the processes running bash, list all processes and pipe through **grep**.
    ps -ef | grep bash

    e. n/a

    f. List the current shell processes including the PID, PPID, owner, and command.
    ps -opid,ppid,user,comm

4. A hung process might be terminated by sending it a signal using the **kill** utility (Sobell, page 470).

    a. n/a

    b. Find the PID using **ps** and then terminate the process using **kill** with the default TERM signal.
    ps
    kill *PID*

    c. Open another terminal window and determine the process ID of the bash process running in the terminal window.
    CONTROL-N
    ps

    d. Use **kill** to terminate this bash process. Try a TERM signal first. Did that work? Which signal will force the termination of the process?
    kill -KILL *PID*

5. Modify the report.sh script from Chapter 9 to also list all the bash processes running on the system. Set up the command to display the owner, PID, terminal (TTY), and command.
    ps -e -ouser,pid,tty,comm | grep bash

6. Working as **student**, use **crontab** to schedule report.sh to run every Mon/Wed/Fri at 8am (Sobell, User crontab files, page 612).
    crontab -e
    add a line that reads:
    0 8 * * 1,3,5 /home/student/bin/report.sh

7. Have Max issue a command to back up his home directory.

    a. Use tar to create the file /tmp/max_home.tar.
    tar cvf /tmp/max_home.tar ~

    b. Modify the tar command to add gzip compression and name the file /tmp/max_home.tgz.

tar czvf /tmp/max_home.tgz ~

c. Modify the command so the output filename includes the current date using command substitution (Sobell, page 351). (Hint: The command **date +%Y%m%d** will provide a nicely formatted date.)
    tar czvf /tmp/max_home-$(date +%Y%m%d).tgz ~

d. Schedule the job to run every Saturday at 10pm.
    crontab -e
    0 10 * * 6 tar czvf /tmp/max_home-$(date +%Y%m%d).tgz ~

Chapter 16, Lab 2: Growing Filesystems Using LVM (10–15 minutes)

Learning Objectives and Outcomes:
Use LVM and filesystem resizing tools to increase the size of the partition mounted at /home.

Required Setup and Tools:

- Fedora Linux 15 installation with an ordinary user (student) and the root password

Additional Resources:

- Sobell, Chapter 3, page 42, LVM

- Sobell, Chapter 12

- Sobell, Chapter 16

Recommended Procedures:

1. Display the size of /home using df -h /home.

2. Dislpay the name of the block device hosting /home.

3. Display the size of the LV (logical volume) holding /home by giving the command **lvdisplay** *logicalvolume,* where *logicalvolume* is the device name displayed above.

4. View the size of the VG (volume group) holding the logical volume by giving the command **vgdisplay**. The Free PE /Size numbers are _____.

5. Add 500MB to the logical volume.

6. Use **lvdisplay** and **df** to display the sizes of the LV and the filesystem.

7. Expand the filesystem so that it occupies all newly available space using **resize2fs**.

8. Use **lvdisplay** and **df** to display the sizes of the LV and the filesystem.

Deliverables:
An additional 500MB of space for /home.

CHAPTER 16, LAB 2—SOLUTIONS:

1. Display the size of /home using df -h /home.
   About 2468MB

2. Dislpay the name of the block device hosting /home.
   Varies but may be /dev/mapper/vg_linux-LogVol02 or /dev/mapper/vg_linux-home

3. Display the size of the LV (logical volume) holding /home by giving the command **lvdisplay** *logicalvolume*, where *logicalvolume* is the device name displayed above.
   About 256MB

4. View the size of the VG (volume group) holding the logical volume by giving the command **vgdisplay**. The Free PE /Size numbers are _____
   Varies, perhaps 72 / 2.25GB

5. Add 500MB to the logical volume.
   lvextend -L +500M *logicalvolume*

6. Use **lvdisplay** and **df** to display the sizes of the LV and the filesystem.
   lvdisplay shows about 768MB and df shows 248MB

7. Expand the filesystem so that it occupies all newly available space using **resize2fs**.
   resize2fs *logicalvolume*

8. Use **lvdisplay** and **df** to display the sizes of the LV and the filesystem.
   lvdisplay shows 768MB and df shows 744MB

CHAPTER 16, LAB 3: ADDING A NEW FILESYSTEM (20–30 MINUTES)

LEARNING OBJECTIVES AND OUTCOMES:

You will create a new ext4 filesystem that will be available at /web and will include support for ACLs.

REQUIRED SETUP AND TOOLS:

- Fedora Linux 15 installation with an ordinary user (student) and the root password

ADDITIONAL RESOURCES:

- Sobell, Chapter 3, page 42, LVM

- Sobell, Chapter 12

- Sobell, Chapter 16

RECOMMENDED PROCEDURES:

1. Display the partition table using **parted** (Sobell, page 617).

2. There is no free space for a new partition, however, space is available in the VG (volume group).

3. Use **vgdisplay** to display the Free PE/Size information.

4. What is the name of the VG?

5. Create a new LV (logical volume) named **web** that is approximately 500MB in size.

6. Create an ext4 filesystem on the new LV.

7. Create a directory to use as the mount point.

8. Add an entry to the /etc/fstab file that will mount the new filesystem at boot time (Sobell, page 524).

9. Use **mount -a** to test the syntax of the new fstab entry and **df** or **mount** to confirm the outcome.

10. Compare the default mount options of the new filesystem with /home, which was created during installation.

    a. View the default mount options using **tune2fs -l** *device* | **grep options**.

b. The filesystem created during installation has support for ACLs (Sobell, page 208). Copy the /tmp/campaign files to /web. Note the error message and compare the permissions of the /tmp/campaign and /web/campaign directories.

c. Modify the new filesystem to support ACLs by default.

d. Unmount and remount the new filesystem.

e. Remove the /web/campaign directory and copy the /tmp/campaign files again.

f. View the ACLs of the /web/campaign directory.

DELIVERABLES:

A new filesystem with support for ACLs.

CHAPTER 16, LAB 3—SOLUTIONS:

1. Display the partition table using **parted** (Sobell, page 617).

   parted /dev/sda print

2. n/a

3. n/a

4. What is the name of the VG?

   Varies, but is often vg_*hostname* or may be vg_linux

5. Create a new LV (logical volume) named **web** that is approximately 500MB in size.

   lvcreate -L 500M -n web vg_linux

6. Create an ext4 filesystem on the new LV.

   mkfs -t ext4 /dev/vg_linux/web

7. Create a directory to use as the mount point.

   mkdir /web

8. Add an entry to the /etc/fstab file that will mount the new filesystem at boot time (Sobell, page 524).

   /dev/mapper/vg_linux-web /web ext4 defaults 1 2

9. n/a

10. Compare the default mount options of the new filesystem with /home, which was created during installation.

    a. View the default mount options using **tune2fs -l** *device* **| grep options**.

       tune2fs -l /dev/mapper/vg_linux-LogVol02 | grep options

       tune2fs -l /dev/mapper/vg_linux-web | grep options

    b. The filesystem created during installation has support for ACLs (Sobell, page 208). Copy the /tmp/campaign files to /web. Note the error message and compare the permissions of the /tmp/campaign and /web/campaign directories.

       cp -a /tmp/campaign /web

       getfacl /tmp/campaign

       getfacl /web/campaign

    c. Modify the new filesystem to support ACLs by default.

       tune2fs -o acl /dev/mapper/vg_linux-web

    d. Unmount and remount the new filesystem.

       umount /web

       mount /web

e.   Remove the /web/campaign directory and copy the /tmp/campaign files again.

rm -rf /web/campaign

cp -a /tmp/campaign /web

f.   View the ACLs of the /web/campaign directory.

getfacl /web/campaign

CHAPTER 17, LAB 1: VIEWING THE CURRENT CONFIGURATION (5–10 MINUTES)

LEARNING OBJECTIVES AND OUTCOMES:

Verify the current network settings.

REQUIRED SETUP AND TOOLS:

- Fedora Linux 15 installation with an ordinary user (student) and the root password

- Access to the classroom server or other system on the same network for testing connectivity

ADDITIONAL RESOURCES:

- Sobell, Chapter 17

- Sobell, Chapter 10

RECOMMENDED PROCEDURES:

1. GUI: Right-click the network icon and select Connection Information. Record you current connection information.

   a. Interface: _Ethernet (p3p1)_

   b. IP Address: _192.168.100.85_

   c. Subnet Mask: _255.255.255.0_

   d. Default Route: _192.168.100.2_

   e. Primary DNS: _192.168.100.1_

2. CLI: Type the following commands to view the current connection information.

   a. **ip addr**

   b. **ip addr show eth0**

   c. **ip route**

   d. **hostname**

   e. **cat /etc/resolv.conf**

3. View the following files. (Which command shows the contents of a text file?)

   a. /etc/sysconfig/network-scripts/ifcfg-eth0
      Cat

   b. /etc/sysconfig/network
      Cat

c.　/etc/resolv.conf

　　　　　　cat

　　　d.　/etc/hosts

　　　　　　cat

4.　Is the eth0 interface configured using a static address or DHCP?

　　　　　　yes

DELIVERABLES:

A list of the current TCP/IP network settings.

CHAPTER 17, LAB 1—SOLUTIONS:

1. n/a

2. n/a

3. Which command shows the contents of a text file?
   cat or less

4. Is the eth0 interface configured using a static address or DHCP?
   Unless instructed otherwise in the Chapter 3 installation labs, your system should be getting an address using DHCP.

Chapter 17, Lab 2: Configuring Static IP Addresses (10–20 minutes)

Learning Objectives and Outcomes:

In preparation to set up this system as a server, you will configure the system to use a static address.

Required Setup and Tools:

- Fedora Linux 15 installation with an ordinary user (student) and the root password

- Access to the classroom server or other system on the same network for testing connectivity

Additional Resources:

- Sobell, Chapter 17

- Sobell, Chapter 10

Recommended Procedures:

Note: This section will configure a static address. Make sure you do *not* set up your system's IP address so it conflicts with (is the same as) another system on your network.

Option 1: (for students in a NAT or Host only environment with access to the class server image locally):

Edit files to add a static network configuration. Use the text sample of ifcfg-Auto_eth0 file as a guide (Sobell, page 654).

1. Copy the /etc/sysconfig/network-scripts/ifcfg-eth0 file to create an ifcfg-eth0:0 file.

2. Edit the new ifcfg-eth0:0 file to use the following settings.

   a. Device: eth0:0

   b. NM_CONTROLLED: no

   c. IP Address: 172.18.0.50

   d. Netmask: 255.255.255.0

   e. Start at boot time

3. Add an /etc/hosts entry for 172.18.0.254 server.example.com server srv (Sobell, page 380).

4. Add an /etc/hosts entry for your ip and hostname.

5. Start the interface using **ifup eth0:0**.

6. Test

   a. View the configuration using **ip addr**.

   b. Ping the class server by IP address and name.

To make both networks available at boot time, you need to disable NetworkManager and enable the legacy network scripts that can handle more complex network configurations.

7. Edit the /etc/sysconfig/network-scripts/ifcfg-eth0 file so that NM_CONTROLLED is set to NO and verify the interface will start ONBOOT.

8. Issue the following commands (more on these commands at the end of this lab).

   a. **systemctl disable NetworkManager.service**

   b. **systemctl enable network.service**

9. Reboot your system and check your network settings.

Option 2: If you are on an isolated machine, simply change the ifcfg-eth0 file from DHCP to static using the same IP Address, netmask, router, and DNS servers you discovered in Chapter 17, Lab 1, step 1 or 2.

Option 3: If you are on physical machines in a lab, or using bridged virtual machines, check with your instructor or network administrator to obtain the correct network information.

DELIVERABLES:

A system that is configured with a static network address and that can communicate with the classroom server.

Chapter 17, Lab 2—SOLUTIONS:

1. Copy the /etc/sysconfig/network-scripts/ifcfg-eth0 file to create an ifcfg-eth0:0 file.

   cp /etc/sysconfig/network-scripts/ifcfg-eth0 /etc/sysconfig/network-scripts/ifcfg-eth0:0

2. Edit the new ifcfg-eth0:0 file to use the following settings.

   a. Device: eth0:0
      DEVICE=eth0:0

   b. NM_CONTROLLED: no
      NM_CONTROLLED=no

   c. IP Address: 172.18.0.50
      IPADDR=172.18.0.50

   d. Netmask: 255.255.255.0
      NETMASK=255.255.255.0

   e. Start at boot time
      ONBOOT=yes

3. n/a

4. Add an /etc/hosts entry for your ip and hostname.
   172.18.0.50 linux.example.com linux

5. n/a

6. Test

   a. n/a

   b. Ping the class server by IP address and name.
      ping -c3 172.18.0.254
      ping -c3 server.example.com.
      Ping -c1 srv

7.–9. n/a

CHAPTER 17, LAB 3: TROUBLESHOOTING NETWORK CONNECTIONS (5–10 MINUTES)

LEARNING OBJECTIVES AND OUTCOMES:
Test and troubleshoot network connections.

REQUIRED SETUP AND TOOLS:

- Fedora Linux 15 installation with an ordinary user (student) and the root password

- Access to the classroom server or other system on the same network for testing connectivity

ADDITIONAL RESOURCES:

- Sobell, Chapter 17

- Sobell, Chapter 10

RECOMMENDED PROCEDURES:

1. Use **ping** to test your new connection (Sobell, page 386).

   a. Can you **ping** your own IP Address?

   b. Can you **ping** the class server by name? If not, then by IP?

   c. Optional: If you have a router, can you **ping** the router? Can you **ping** an address beyond the router?

2. Compare the output of hostname resolution tools (Sobell, page 388 and throughout Chapter 24).

   a. Use **host** to determine the IP address of www.fedoraproject.org.

   b. Use **dig** to determine the IP address of www.fedoraproject.org.

   c. Try using **host** or **dig** to determine the IP address of srv. (This test should fail.)

   d. Give the command **getent hosts srv** to determine the IP address of your server using the hosts file.

3. Verify your IP Address and netmask using the **ip** utility.

4. Check routing information using the **ip** utility.

5. Optional: If you have Internet connectivity, use **traceroute** to display the path a packet takes from your system to www.fedoraproject.org (Sobell, page 387).

Deliverables:

A system configured with a static network address that can communicate with the classroom server.

CHAPTER 17, LAB 3—SOLUTIONS:

1. Use **ping** to test your new connection (Sobell, page 386).

   a. Can you **ping** your own IP Address?
   ping -c3 172.18.0.50

   b. Can you **ping** the class server by name? If not, then by IP?
   ping -c3 server.example.com
   ping -c3 172.18.0.254

   c. Optional: If you have a router, can you **ping** the router? Can you **ping** an address beyond the router?
   Use the router address you recorded in Chapter 17, Lab 1.

2. Compare the output of hostname resolution tools (Sobell, page 388 and throughout Chapter 24).

   a. Use **host** to determine the IP address of www.fedoraproject.org.
   host www.fedoraproject.org

   b. Use **dig** to determine the IP address of www.fedoraproject.org.
   dig www.fedoraproject.org

   c. Try using **host** or **dig** to determine the IP address of srv. (This test should fail.)
   host srv
   Host srv not found: 3(NXDOMAIN)

   d. Give the command **getent hosts srv** to determine the IP address of your server using the hosts file.
   172.18.0.254

3. Verify your IP Address and netmask using the **ip** utility.
   ip addr show eth0

4. Check routing information using the **ip** utility.
   ip route

5. Optional: If you have Internet connectivity, use **traceroute** to display the path a packet takes from your system to www.fedoraproject.org (Sobell, page 387).
   traceroute www.fedoraproject.org

CHAPTER 18, LAB 1: USING SSH FOR REMOTE SYSTEM ADMINISTRATION (10–15 MINUTES)

LEARNING OBJECTIVES AND OUTCOMES:

In this lab you will use the **ssh** utility to connect to a remote system and perform system administration tasks.

REQUIRED SETUP AND TOOLS:

- Fedora Linux 15 installation with an ordinary user (student) and the root password

- Access to the classroom server

- Note the Class Server name, IP address, and available user account and password

  o server.example.com

  o 172.18.0.254

  o mark/P@$$w0rd

ADDITIONAL RESOURCES:

- Sobell, Chapter 18

RECOMMENDED PROCEDURES:

1. Make a note of the hostname or IP address of the classroom server and the username/password available to you for this lab.
   Unless otherwise specified by the instructor:
   server.example.com, 172.18.0.254, and mark/P@$$word

2. Use **ssh** to connect to the classroom server (Sobell, JumpStart on page 677).

   ssh mark @ server

   a. Use the **w** utility to see who is connected and where the connection originated (Sobell, page 168). Try these commands and look for your connection:

      w

      who am i

   b. Determine the amount of free memory on the server in MB.

      free -m   171 free

   c. Attempt to run a graphical application such as **system-config-printer**. What happens when the -X option is not used with the ssh connection?

      opend printhgfail   will not open display
      message if the -x option   with no ssh connection
      localhost

   d. Exit the ssh session.

      ext

3. Connect to the class server, run the system-config-printer command, and exit immediately when finished.

ssh -x mark@server system-config-printer

DELIVERABLES:

You should be able to use **ssh** to access a remote system using passwords.

CHAPTER 18, LAB 1—SOLUTIONS:

1. n/a

2. Use **ssh** to connect to the classroom server (Sobell, JumpStart on page 677).
   ssh mark@server

   a. n/a

   b. Determine the amount of free memory on the server in MB.
      free -m

   c. Attempt to run a graphical application such as **system-config-printer**. What happens when the -X option is not used with the ssh connection?
      The application will fail to start with a "cannot open display" message if the -X option was not used with the ssh connection.

   d. Exit the ssh session.
      exit

3. Connect to the class server, run the system-config-printer command, and exit immediately when finished.
   ssh -X mark@server system-config-printer

Chapter 18, Lab 2: Transferring Files Securely Using scp and rsync (20–30 minutes)

Learning Objectives and Outcomes:

In this lab you will use scp and rsync to securely transfer files between systems. Then you will automate these procedures using OpenSSH keys.

Required Setup and Tools:

- Fedora Linux 15 installation with an ordinary user account (student)

- Access to the classroom server

- Note the Class Server name, IP address, and available user account and password.

  - server.example.com

  - 172.18.0.254

  - mark/P@$$w0rd

Additional Resources:

- Sobell, Chapter 18

Recommended Procedures:

Transfer files securely.

1. Copy your local /etc/hosts file to the classroom server and place it in the /tmp directory with a name of **hosts-***name* (replace *name* with your name or initials).

   scp /etc/hosts mark@server:/tmp/hosts-name

2. Copy the classroom server /etc/hosts file to your local home directory.

   scp mark@server:/etc/hosts ~

3. Use **rsync** to copy the system activity monitoring script from Chapter 9, Lab 2 to Mark's account on the remote system.

   rsync -l bin/report.sh mark@sever:

4. Run the system monitoring script on the remote system. (Hint: Do not forget to make it executable and specify the pathname of the executable file.)

   ssh mark@sever 'chmod 775 report.sh; ./report.sh'

Use authorized key authentication with OpenSSH.

5. Create an ssh key pair for your local user with an empty password (Sobell, page 689).

   ssh-keygen

6. Use **ssh-copy-id** to copy the public key in the account of the remote user (Sobell, page 690).

    ssh-keygen

7. Test connectivity by using **ssh** to connect to the remote host. No password should be required.

    ssh mark@sover 'hostname'

8. Return to the local system and change the passphrase on your private key to **password**.

    ssh-keygen-P

9. To test the new passphrase, **ssh-agent** must forget the passphrase. Log out of the Fedora graphical desktop, then log in again as the same user and then use **ssh** to connect to the class server. You should be prompted for the ssh passphrase the first time you connect.

10. Return to the local system and then reconnect to the remote system. You should not be asked for the passphase the second time.

DELIVERABLES:

You should be able to transfer files securely and use **ssh** to access a remote system using passwords or authorized keys.

Chapter 18, Lab 2—SOLUTIONS:

1. Copy your local /etc/hosts file to the classroom server and place it in the /tmp directory with a name of hosts-*name* (replace *name* with your name or initials).
   scp /etc/hosts mark@server:/tmp/hosts-*name*

2. Copy the classroom server /etc/hosts file to your local home directory.
   scp mark@server:/etc/hosts ~

3. Use **rsync** to copy the system activity monitoring script from Chapter 9, Lab 2 to Mark's account on the remote system.
   rsync ~/bin/report.sh mark@server:

4. Run the system monitoring script on the remote system. (Hint: Do not forget to make it executable and specify the pathname of the executable file.)
   ssh mark@server 'chmod 755 report.sh; ./report.sh'

5. Create an ssh key pair for your local user with an empty password (Sobell, page 689).
   ssh-keygen

6. Use **ssh-copy-id** to copy the public key in the account of the remote user (Sobell, page 690).
   ssh-copy-id mark@server

7. Test connectivity by using **ssh** to connect to the remote host. No password should be required.
   ssh mark@server **'hostname'**

8. Return to the local system and change the passphrase on your private key to **password**.
   ssh-keygen -p

9. n/a

10. n/a

Chapter 18, Lab 3: Configuring the OpenSSH Server to Accept Connections (15–20 minutes)

Learning Objectives and Outcomes:

In this lab you will configure OpenSSH to accept connections.

Required Setup and Tools:

- Fedora Linux 15 installation with an ordinary user account (student)

- Access to the classroom server

- Note the Class Server name, IP address, and available user account and password.

  o server.example.com

  o 172.18.0.254

  o mark/P@$$w0rd

Additional Resources:

- Sobell, Chapter 18

Recommended Procedures:

Configure OpenSSH server to accept connections.

1. Ensure **sshd** is running and set up to start when the system boots.

   systemctl status sshd.service   *chk config --list sshd*
   systemctl is enable sshd.service   *is active*

2. Attempt to connect from the remote classroom server back to your own system.

   ssh mark@172.18.0.50

3. Troubleshooting: If the connection is refused, check that the firewall is disabled (or ssh port 22 is allowed) on your local system using **System à Administration à Firewall**.

4. Secure **sshd** so root cannot log in; allow only ordinary users to connect.

   a. Test to see if root can use **ssh** to connect to your system.

   ssh root@172.18.0.50

   b. Locally, working with root privileges, edit the /etc/ssh/sshd_config file.

   su -
   vi /etc/ssh/sshd-config

   c. Find the PermitRootLogin line, uncomment it, and change the **yes** to a **no**.

   permitRootLogin yes
   ↑r
   PermitRootLogin no

5. After saving the changes, restart the ssh server.

   systemctl restart sshd.service

6. Troubleshooting: Ensure SELinux is in permissive mode using **system-config-selinux**.

7. Test your connection from the remote system. You should not be able to connect directly as root. Mark should still be able to connect (and use **su** to gain root privileges).

8. Troubleshooting: Ensure the firewall is disabled or open for port 22 to allow ssh traffic.

DELIVERABLES:

Your system should act as an ssh server that permits only non-root accounts to authenticate (log in).

Chapter 18, Lab 3—SOLUTIONS:

1. Ensure **sshd** is running and set up to start when the system boots.

    systemctl status sshd.service

    systemctl is-enabled sshd.service

    chkconfig --list sshd

2. Attempt to connect from the remote classroom server back to your own system.

    ssh mark@172.18.0.50

3. n/a

4. Secure **sshd** so root cannot log in; allow only ordinary users to connect.

    a. Test to see if root can use **ssh** to connect to your system.

        (From the classroom server:) **ssh root@172.18.0.50**

    b. Locally, working with root privileges, edit the /etc/ssh/sshd_config file.

        su -

        vi /etc/ssh/sshd_config

    c. Find the PermitRootLogin line, uncomment it, and change the **yes** to a **no**.

        change

        #PermitRootLogin yes

        to

        PermitRootLogin no

5. After saving the changes, restart the ssh server.

    systemctl restart sshd.service

6.–8. n/a

Chapter 19, Lab 1: Explore FTP Client Utilities (10–20 minutes)

Learning Objectives and Outcomes:

You will explore FTP client utilities.

Required Setup and Tools:

- Fedora Linux 15 installation with an ordinary user (student) and the root password

- Access to the classroom server

- Access to the Fedora installation DVD or DVD iso file to install required packages

Additional Resources:

- Sobell, Chapter 19

Recommended Procedures:

1. Preparation: Use **touch** to create a file named **memo** in your local home directory. You will copy this file to the remote system.

2. Follow the FTP JumpStart I tutorial on Sobell, page 704. Connect to server.example.com as the user **mark** with a password of **P@$$w0rd**.

   a. Connect to the server and authenticate as mark.

   b. List the available files.

   c. Get the class-info file.

   d. Copy the memo file to the remote host.

3. Put a copy of your /etc/hosts file into Mark's home directory on the server.

   a. Which error do you get when you issue the **put /etc/hosts** command?

   b. Try giving a destination filename.

   c. You can also use two commands: Change your local working directory and then copy the file.

4. Close the connection to server.example.com.

5. Explore an anonymous connection.

   a. Connect to server.example.com and log in as the user named **anonymous**. Traditionally the password is your email address. Pressing ENTER without entering a password also works.

   b. Issue the command **ls /**. What files are in the root directory?

   c. Change to the pub/LDIFs directory.

   d. Without leaving the connection, create a local ~/ldifs subdirectory and transfer all the LDIF files to this subdirectory.

   e. If you get prompted, answer **no**. Turn off prompting and attempt the transfer again.

6. Use lftp to connect an anonymous to server.example.com.

   a. Did you have to give a username and password?

   b. List the contents of the pub/LDIFs directory.

   c. Press the UP ARROW key to display the command history.

   d. Use TAB completion to get the example-ca.crt file.

   e. Type **quit** to exit.

DELIVERABLES:

The class-info file copied to the local system, the memo file copied to the remote system, and the LDIF files copied to the local system,

CHAPTER 19, LAB 1—SOLUTIONS:

1. Preparation: Use **touch** to create a file named **memo** in your local home directory. You will copy this file to the remote system.

   touch ~/memo

2. Follow the FTP JumpStart I tutorial on Sobell, page 704. Connect to server.example.com as the user **mark** with a password of **P@$$w0rd**.

   a. Connect to the server and authenticate as mark.

      ftp server.example.com

   b. List the available files.

      ls

   c. Get the class-info file.

      get class-info

   d. Copy the memo file to the remote host.

      put memo

4. Put a copy of your /etc/hosts file into Mark's home directory on the server.

   a. Which error do you get when you issue the **put /etc/hosts** command?

      550 /ctc/hosts: No such file or directory

   b. Try giving a destination filename.

      put /etc/hosts hosts

   c. You can also use two commands: Change your local working directory and then copy the file.

      lcd /etc

      put hosts

4. Close the connection to server.example.com.

   quit

5. Explore an anonymous connection.

   a. n/a

   b. Issue the command **ls /**. What files are in the root directory?

      Only the pub directory. Anonymous ftp sets up a chroot environment (Sobell, page 717).

   c. Change to the pub/LDIFs directory.

      cd pub/LDIFs

   d. Without leaving the connection, create a local ~/ldifs subdirectory and transfer all the LDIF files to this subdirectory.

      !mkdir ~/ldifs

      lcd ~/ldifs

      mget *

e. If you get prompted, answer **no**. Turn off prompting and attempt the transfer again.

prompt

mget *

6. Use lftp to connect an anonymous to server.example.com.

    lftp server.example.com

    a. Did you have to give a username and password?

        No

    b. List the contents of the pub/LDIFs directory.

        ls pub/LDIFs

    c. n/a

    d. Use TAB completion to get the example-ca.crt file.

        get pub/exTAB

    e. n/a

Chapter 19, Lab 2: Configuring an FTP Server (10–20 minutes)

Learning Objectives and Outcomes:

You will set up an FTP server.

Required Setup and Tools:

- Fedora Linux 15 installation with an ordinary user (student) and the root password

- Access to the classroom server

- Access to the Fedora installation DVD or DVD ISO image file to install required packages

Additional Resources:

- Sobell, Chapter 19

Recommended Procedures:

1. Working with root privileges, install the **vsftpd** package.

2. Working with root privileges, enable the **vsftpd** daemon to start at boot time and start it now with the default configuration file.

3. Add content to the /var/ftp/pub directory. For example, copy the /etc/sysconfig/network file to the /var/ftp/pub directory.

4. Test: Connect to your own server as a local user and as anonymous (Sobell, Chapter 19 JumpStart II and Troubleshooting, page 713)

5. Troubleshooting: Ensure that the firewall is disabled or the FTP ports (21/tcp and 21/udp) are open using **system-config-firewall**.

6. Troubleshooting: SELinux may block the FTP service from accessing home directories. If Mark cannot connect or cannot list the contents of his home directory, ensure that SELinux is in permissive mode by giving the command **setenfore permissive**. Alternatively, you can issue the command **setsebool -P ftp_home_dir on** to enable access to the home directories.

7. Secure the FTP server by disabling local logins. Allow only anonymous connections.

    a. Use **rpm** queries to determine the config file for the **vsftpd** package.

b. Edit the vsftpd config file and modify the local_enable parameter.

c. Restart the **vsftpd** daemon.

d. Test: Anonymous should still be able to connect. A user such as Mark should get a Login Failed message.

DELIVERABLES:

An FTP server offering public content for anonymous connections.

Chapter 19, Lab 2—SOLUTIONS:

1. Working with root privileges, install the **vsftpd** package.

   yum install vsftpd

2. Working with root privileges, enable the **vsftpd** daemon to start at boot time and start it now with the default configuration file.

   systemctl enable vsftpd.service

   systemctl start vsftpd.service

3. Add content to the /var/ftp/pub directory. For example, copy the /etc/sysconfig/network file to the /var/ftp/pub directory.

   cp /etc/sysconfig/network /var/ftp/pub

4. n/a

5. n/a

6. n/a

7. Secure the FTP server by disabling local logins. Allow only anonymous connections.

   a. Use **rpm** queries to determine the config file for the **vsftpd** package.

      rpm -qc vsftpd

   b. Edit the vsftpd config file and modify the local_enable parameter.

      Edit the /etc/vsftpd/vsftpd.conf file.

      Change local_enable=YES to local_enable=NO

   c. Restart the **vsftpd** daemon.

      systemctl restart vsftpd

   d. n/a

CHAPTER 19, LAB 3: ADDING A DROPBOX (15–20 MINUTES)

LEARNING OBJECTIVES AND OUTCOMES:

You will set up an FTP server with an incoming dropbox. Anonymous users will be able to upload files to the dropbox, but will not be able to see what is in the dropbox and will not be able to download files from the dropbox.

REQUIRED SETUP AND TOOLS:

- Fedora Linux 15 installation with an ordinary user (student) and the root password

- Access to the Fedora installation DVD or DVD ISO image file to install required packages

ADDITIONAL RESOURCES:

- Sobell, Chapter 19

RECOMMENDED PROCEDURES:

1. Edit the vsftpd config file to allow anonymous users to upload files to the FTP server. Use the comments in the config file, the vsftpd.conf man page, and Sobell, pages 715–725, to determine the values for the following parameters:

   a. anon_upload_enable

   b. anon_umask

   c. chown_uploads

   d. chown_username

2. Create a dropbox directory as /var/ftp/dropbox.

3. Set the permissions and ownership on the dropbox directory. Mark or root should own the directory. The group named **ftp** should have write and execute access but not read access. Other users should have no access.

4. Restart the **vsftpd** daemon.

5. Test:

   a. Can a user connect as anonymous and copy a file to the dropbox directory?

   b. Can anonymous view the contents of the dropbox directory?

   c. Exit from the FTP session and, working as mark or root, view the contents of the dropbox directory. What are the permissions and ownership of the uploaded files?

DELIVERABLES:

An FTP server hosting a dropbox for content contributions.

Chapter 19, Lab 3—SOLUTIONS:

1. Edit the vsftpd config file to allow anonymous users to upload files to the FTP server. Use the comments in the config file, the vsftpd.conf man page, and Sobell, pages 715–725, to determine the values for the following parameters:

   a. anon_upload_enable

      uncomment the line:

      anon_upload_enable=YES

   b. anon_umask

      add the line:

      anon_umask=077

   c. chown_uploads

      uncomment the line:

      chown_uploads=YES

   d. chown_username

      uncomment and modify the username:

      chown_username=mark

2. Create a dropbox directory as /var/ftp/dropbox.

   mkdir /var/ftp/dropbox

3. Set the permissions and ownership on the dropbox directory. Mark or root should own the directory. The group named **ftp** should have write and execute access but not read access. Other users should have no access.

   chown mark:ftp /var/ftp/dropbox

   chmod 730 /var/ftp/dropbox

4. Restart the **vsftpd** daemon.

   systemctl restart vsftpd.service

5. Test:

   a. Can a user connect as anonymous and copy a file to the dropbox directory?

      Yes

   b. Can anonymous view the contents of the dropbox directory?

      No

   c. Exit from the FTP session and, working as mark or root, view the contents of the dropbox directory. What are the permissions and ownership of the uploaded files?

      Owner is mark. Group is ftp. Permissions are 600.

Chapter 20, Lab 1: Setting up sendmail and Dovecot (30–40 minutes)

Learning Objectives and Outcomes:

You will configure and use sendmail and Dovecot for email services.

Required Setup and Tools:

- Fedora Linux 15 installation with an ordinary user (student) and the root password

- Access to the classroom server

Additional Resources:

- Sobell, Chapter 20

Recommended Procedures:

Use the **mutt** utility to read local mail and to send mail.

1. As an ordinary user (student or mark, for example), issue the command **mutt**.

2. The first time you use mutt, you will be prompted to set up the mailbox; press RETURN to create the Mail folder.

3. While using mutt you can highlight any message and press RETURN to read the highlighted message or press **m** to create a new mail message. Send a message to max.

4. Use the menu at the top of the screen to try other options.

5. From the primary (inbox) screen of mutt, type **q** to quit.

Set up a script that sends email using the **mailx** utility.

6. The older **mailx** utility is easy to use in a script that sends email. Create a script that mails the /etc/hosts file to root@localhost with a subject of **tests hosts** and the /etc/sysconfig/network file to mark@linux.example.com with a subject of **test user mail**.

    cat /etc/hosts | mailx -s "test host") root @ local host
    mail -s test user mail") mark@linux < /etc/sysconfig/network

Configure an alias so that root's mail is sent to Mark and Max (Sobell, pages 736–737).

7. Ensure that all mail for root is sent to both Mark and Max.
    working with root privileges, edit the /etc/aliases file and add a line to end of the file root: mark map

8. Restart **sendmail**.
    systemctl restart sendmail.service.

9. Troubleshooting: Ensure that SELinux is in permissive mode by using the SELinux configuration utility (**system-config-selinux**).

10. Test: Send mail to root and check the mail for Mark and Max.

Configure sendmail to receive mail (Sobell, JumpStart II, page 734).

11. Working with root privileges, edit the /etc/mail/sendmail.mc file.

12. Locate the DAEMON_OPTIONS line referencing 127.0.0.1 and comment it out by placing **dnl** at the beginning of the line. Alternatively, you can remove the Addr portion of the line.

13. Restart **sendmail**.

    Systemctl restart sendmail.service

14. Troubleshooting: Ensure the firewall is disabled, or open port 25 to allow SMTP traffic.

15. Test: Connect to the class server and send mail back to mark@linux.

Configure Dovecot (Sobell, Chapter 20, page 754).

16. Start the Dovecot server.

    Systemctl start dovecot.service

17. Set up Dovecot to start when the system boots.

    Systemctl enable dovecot.service

18. Troubleshooting: Ensure the firewall is disabled or open port 993 to allow IMAP traffic.

19. Test: Give the command **mutt -f** imaps://mark@linux or configure Evolution or Thunderbird as an IMAP client.

DELIVERABLES:

A system where all mail sent to root also gets sent to Mark and Max, a system that will receive email from other systems, and a system that hosts an IMAP server for users to read mail.

CHAPTER 20, LAB 1—SOLUTIONS:

1. n/a

2. n/a

3. n/a

4. n/a

5. n/a

6. The older **mailx** utility is easy to use in a script that sends email. Create a script that mails the /etc/hosts file to root@localhost with a subject of **tests hosts** and the /etc/sysconfig/network file to mark@linux.example.com with a subject of **test user mail.**
   cat /etc/hosts | mailx -s "test hosts" root@localhost
   mailx -s "test user mail" mark@linux < /etc/sysconfig/network

7. Ensure that all mail for root is sent to both Mark and Max.
   Working with root privileges, edit the /etc/aliases file and add a line to the end of the file:
   root: mark max

8. Restart **sendmail.**
   systemctl restart sendmail.service

9. n/a

10. n/a

11. n/a

12. n/a

13. Restart **sendmail.**
    systemctl restart sendmail.service

14. n/a

15. n/a

16. Start the Dovecot server.
    systemctl start dovecot.service

17. Set up Dovecot to start when the system boots.
    systemctl enable dovecot.service

18. n/a

19. n/a

Chapter 21, Lab 1: Configuring Access to Centralized User Accounts (10–20 minutes)

Learning Objectives and Outcomes:

You will use directory services on a network and configure Linux to use LDAP.

Required Setup and Tools:

- Fedora Linux 15 installation with an ordinary user (student) and the root password

- Access to the Fedora installation DVD or DVD ISO image file to install required client packages

- Optional: An NIS or Openldap server to connect to as a client; obtain information about these servers from your network administrator or instructor

Additional Resources:

- Sobell, Chapter 21, pages 776–788, LDAP

Recommended Procedures:

If your network administrator or instructor can provide you with valid NIS or LDAP configuration information, enter that information. You will need:

- LDAP server hostname: _____

- Base DN: _____

- Location of CA Certificate: _____

- Username and password to test with:_____

Otherwise, imagine that the classroom server offers accounts through LDAP and view the configuration file changes rather than testing with an actual login process.

1. Open the Authentication Configuration window and enter the root password when prompted.

2. Change the User Account Database to LDAP.

3. Enter **dc=example,dc=com** as the Search Base DN.

4. Enter **server.example.com** as the LDAP Server.

5. Change the Authentication Method to LDAP password.

6. Check the box for TLS encryption.

7. Download the CA Certificate from ftp://server.example.com/pub/example-ca.crt.

8. Apply your changes.

9. View the following files and look for references to the settings just configured:

   a. /etc/openldap/ldap.conf

   b. /etc/openldap/cacerts/*

   c. /etc/sssd/sssd.conf

   d. /etc/nsswitch.conf

   e. /etc/sysconfig/authconfig

DELIVERABLES:

A system configured as a client for LDAP authentication.

CHAPTER 21, LAB 1—SOLUTIONS:

1. Open the Authentication Configuration window and enter the root password when prompted.

   Applicationsà Otherà Authentication

   or, from the command line

   system-config-authentication

2. n/a

3. n/a

4. n/a

5. n/a

6. n/a

7. n/a

8. n/a

9. n/a

Chapter 21, Lab 2: Configuring an LDAP Server (30–45 minutes)

Learning Objectives and Outcomes:

You will use the directory services on a network and configure Linux to use LDAP.

Required Setup and Tools:

- Fedora Linux 15 installation with an ordinary user (student) and the root password

- Access to the Fedora installation DVD or DVD iso file to install required client packages

- Internet access to the Fedora repository to install required server packages

- Access to the classroom server to download sample LDIF files

Additional Resources:

- Sobell, Chapter 21, pages 776–788, LDAP

Recommended Procedures:

1. Pick a suffix to use for your server. The text uses **dc=brillserve,dc=com**.

2. Install the openldap server and client packages. You will need to enable the Fedora repository to install the server component.

3. Follow the "Step-by-Step Setup" steps in Sobell, page 779.

4. Start, enable, and test your server.

5. Create and import the one.ldif file as described in Sobell, page 781, but use your base DN.

6. Additional LDIF files are available on the classroom server in the /var/ftp/pub/LDIFs directory. This directory can be accessed using FTP, HTTP, NFS, or ssh (as mark). Copy the LDIF files from the classroom server.

7. Modify the LDIF files to match your suffix.

8. Import your modified LDIF files using various methods:

    a. Use **ldapmodify** to import the base.ldif file.

b. Use **ldapadd** to import the users.ldif files.

c. Use **ldapadd** to import the group.ldif file. Have **ldapadd** prompt for the password instead of giving it on the command line.

9. Add a telephone number for user1.

10. Add a telephone number and a home phone for user2.

11. Add a Sam the Great employee as specified in the text using the four.ldif file (Sobell, page 784).

12. Add another employee of your choice.

13. Delete the entry for Sam the Great.

14. Optional: Look at the /etc/openldap/schema/core.schema file and the definition for the objectclass organizationalPerson. How might you add mailing address information for your employee?

15. Optional: Configure the Evolution mail reader to use your LDAP server for address book information by following the steps in Sobell, page 785.

DELIVERABLES:

An Openldap server with several entries.

Chapter 21, Lab 2—Solutions:

1. n/a

2. Install the openldap server and client packages. You will need to enable the Fedora repository to install the server component.

   yum install openldap-clients

   yum --enablerepo=fedora install openldap-servers

3. n/a

4. Start, enable, and test your server.

   systemctl start slapd.service

   systemctl enable slapd.service

   ldapsearch -x -s base namingContexts

5. Create and import the one.ldif file as described in Sobell, page 781, but use your base DN.

   dn: dc=brillserve,dc=com

   changetype: add

   dc: brillserve

   objectClass: dcObject

   objectClass: organization

   organizationName: Zbrill Associates

   ldapmodify -xD "cn=ldapadmin,dc=brillserve,dc=com" -w porcupine -f one.ldif

6. Additional LDIF files are available on the classroom server in the /var/ftp/pub/LDIFs directory. This directory can be accessed using FTP, HTTP, NFS, or ssh (as mark). Copy the LDIF files from the classroom server.

   rsync -av mark@server.example.com:/var/ftp/pub/LDIF* .

   [You can also use ftp or http to get the files.]

7. Modify the LDIF files to match your suffix.

   One way to modify the files is to use **vi** with a search and replace string:**%s/dc=example/dc=brillserve/gc**

8. Import your modified LDIF files using various methods:

   a. Use **ldapmodify** to import the base.ldif file.

      ldapmodify -xD "cn=ldapadmin,dc=brillserve,dc=com" -w porcupine -f base.ldif

   b. Use **ldapadd** to import the users.ldif files.

      ldapadd -xD "cn=ldapadmin,dc=brillserve,dc=com" -w porcupine -f users.ldif

   c. Use **ldapadd** to import the group.ldif file. Have **ldapadd** prompt for the password instead of giving it on the command line.

      ldapadd -xD "cn=ldapadmin,dc=brillserve,dc=com" -W -f groups.ldif

9. Add a telephone number for user1.

   The LDIF file should contain:

   dn: uid=user1,ou=People,dc=brillserve,dc=com

   changetype: modify

   add: telephoneNumber

   telephoneNumber: 999 999 0000

10. Add a telephone number and a home phone for user2.

    dn: uid=user2,ou=People,dc=brillserve,dc=com

    changetype: modify

    add: telephoneNumber

    telephoneNumber: 999 999 1111

    -

    add: homePhone

    homePhone: 999 999 1234

11. n/a

12. n/a

13. Delete the entry for Sam the Great.

    You can use an LDIF file such as six.ldif in the text (Sobell, page 784):

    dn: cn=Sam the Great,ou=employees,dc=brillserve,dc=com

    changetype: delete

    then

    ldapmodify -xD "cn=ldapadmin,dc=brillserve,dc=com" -w porcupine -f six.ldif

    or use an **ldapdelete** command:

    ldapdelete -xD "cn=ldapadmin,dc=brillserve,dc=com" -w porcupine cn=Sam the Great,ou=employees,dc=brillserve,dc=com

14. Optional: Look at the /etc/openldap/schema/core.schema file and the definition for the objectclass organizationalPerson. How might you add mailing address information for your employee?

    street: 1234 Broadway

    l: NYC

    st: NY

    postalCode: 12345

15. n/a

Chapter 22, Lab 1: Connecting to Existing NFS Shares (20–30 minutes)

Learning Objectives and Outcomes:

You will configure your system to act as a client to a remote NFS share at startup.

Required Setup and Tools:

- Fedora Linux 15 installation with an ordinary user (student) and the root password

- Access to the classroom server NFS shares

- Access to the Fedora installation DVD or DVD ISO image file to install required packages

Additional Resources:

- Sobell, Chapter 22

Recommended Procedures:

1. The class server has available NFS shares. View the shares that are available.

2. Working with root privileges, make the /var/ftp/pub share on the classroom server available as /nfsmount on the local system.

3. Explore access to the /nfsmount files.

   a. Who owns the files in /nfsmount?

   b. Can Mark read the files? Modify the files? Create or delete a file?

   c. Can root read the files? Modify the files? Create or delete a file?

4. Make the files available at boot time.

   a. Edit the /etc/fstab file to add the line
      server.example.com:/var/ftp/pub /nfsmount NFS defaults 0 0

   b. To test before rebooting, umount the /nfsmount and restart the netfs service.

   c. Reboot your system and ensure the files are available.

5. Connect to the /ldap share on the classroom server; this share is readable and writable. Have the files appear locally in the /nfsrw directory.

6. Explore access to the /nfsrw files.

   a. Who owns the files in /nfsrw?

   b. Can Mark read the files? Modify the files? Create or delete a file?

   c. Can root read the files? Modify the files? Create or delete a file?

DELIVERABLES:

A system acting as a client to a remote NFS share.

CHAPTER 22, LAB 1—SOLUTIONS:

1. The class server has available NFS shares. View the shares that are available.

   showmount -e server.example.com

2. Working with root privileges, make the /var/ftp/pub share on the classroom server available as /nfsmount on the local system.

   su -

   mkdir /nfsmount

   mount server.example.com:/var/ftp/pub /nfsmount

3. Explore access to the /nfsmount files.

   a. Who owns the files in /nfsmount?

      Varies: root, student, or mark

   b. Can Mark read the files? Modify the files? Create or delete a file?

      Mark should be able to read but not modify or create files. The share is read-only.

   c. Can root read the files? Modify the files? Create or delete a file?

      Root should be able to read but nor modify or create files. The share is read-only.

4. Make the files available at boot time.

   a. Edit the /etc/fstab file to add the line

      server.example.com:/var/ftp/pub /nfsmount NFS defaults 0 0

   b. To test before rebooting, umount the /nfsmount and restart the netfs service.

      systemctl restart netfs.service

   c. n/a

5. Connect to the /ldap share on the classroom server; this share is readable and writable. Have the files appear locally in the /nfsrw directory.

   mkdir /nfsrw

   mount server.example.com:/ldap /nfsrw

6. Explore access to the /nfsrw files.

   a. Who owns the files in /nfsrw?

      Varies: root, student, or mark

   b. Can Mark read the files? Modify the files? Create or delete a file?

      Mark can read files and depending on the permissions of the files may be able to modify or create files.

   c. Can root read the files? Modify the files? Create or delete a file?

      root can read files but is "squashed" to appear as the user named nobody when determining permissions. Most likely the other permissions apply.

Chapter 22, Lab 2: Exploring On-Demand Mounting (20–30 minutes)

Learning Objectives and Outcomes:

You will configure your system to act as a client to a remote NFS share that is mounted on demand.

Required Setup and Tools:

- Fedora Linux 15 installation with an ordinary user (student) and the root password

- Access to the classroom server NFS shares

- Access to the Internet to install the required packages

Additional Resources:

- Sobell, Chapter 22, pages 811–814

Recommended Procedures:

1. The classroom server shares account home directories in the /ldap share. Configure your local system to use **autofs** to monitor the /ldap directory and mount the remote user1 and user2 directories on demand.

   a. Install, enable, and start the **autofs** service.

   b. Create the directory to be monitored.

   c. Edit /etc/auto.master to add the following line:
      /ldap   /etc/auto.ldap

   d. Create the /etc/auto.ldap file with the following lines:
      user1   -rw server.example.com:/ldap/user1
      user2   -rw server.example.com:/ldap/user2

2. Assume more users will be added. Modify your configuration to use wildcards.

3. Troubleshooting: SELinux is enabled by default and may block access to home directories both locally or on remote systems. To temporarily disable SELinux, working with root privileges give the command **setenfore=0**. See the nfs_selinux man page for other options.

Deliverables:

A system mounting a remote NFS share on demand.

Chapter 22, Lab 2—SOLUTIONS:

1. The classroom server shares account home directories in the /ldap share. Configure your local system to use **autofs** to monitor the /ldap directory and mount the remote user1 and user2 directories on demand.

    a. Install, enable, and start the **autofs** service.
        yum –enablerepo=fedora install autofs
        systemctl enable autofs.service
        systemctl start autofs.service

    b. Create the directory to be monitored.
        mkdir /ldap

    c. n/a

    d. n/a

2. Assume more users will be added. Modify your configuration to use wildcards.
    *   -rw   server.example.com:/ldap/&

3. n/a

CHAPTER 22, LAB 3: SHARING FILES USING NFS (30–40 MINUTES)

LEARNING OBJECTIVES AND OUTCOMES:

You will create read and read/write NFS shares.

REQUIRED SETUP AND TOOLS:

- Fedora Linux 15 installation with an ordinary user and the root password

- Access to the classroom server NFS shares

- Access to the Fedora installation DVD or DVD ISO image file to install required packages

ADDITIONAL RESOURCES:

- Sobell, Chapter 22

RECOMMENDED PROCEDURES:

Make the yum repository (from Chapter 13, Lab 6) available via NFS. Only allow the 172.18.0.0/24 network to connect to this share.

1. Ensure the necessary packages are installed.

2. Set up the NFS service to start at boot time.

3. Modify the /etc/exports file to share the yum repository (/var/www/html/packages).

4. Start or restart the NFS service.

5. Troubleshooting: Check that the firewall is disabled or the NFS port (2049) is open using **system-config-firewall**.

6. Mount your share to test.

7. Share the /home directory as read/write to the local network.

    a. Edit the /etc/exports file to add the share.

    b. Refresh the export list.

    c. Test your new share.

8. Troubleshooting: SELinux is enabled by default and may block access to home directories both locally or on remote systems. To temporarily disable SELinux, working with root privileges give the command **setenfore=0**. See the nfs_selinux man page for other options.

9. Troubleshooting: Explore the information provided by **exportfs -v** and **rpcinfo -p** (Sobell, pages 809 and 810).

10. Optional: Install and explore the capabilities of the **system-config-nfs** utility (Sobell, JumpStart II, page 802)

DELIVERABLES:

A system acting as a server for a read only and a read/write share.

Chapter 22, Lab 3—SOLUTIONS:

1. Ensure the necessary packages are installed.

   yum list nfs-utils

   yum install nfs-utils

2. Set up the NFS service to start at boot time.

   systemctl enable nfs

3. Modify the /etc/exports file to share the yum repository (/var/www/html/packages).

   /var/www/html/packages 172.18.0.0/24(ro,sync)

4. Start or restart the NFS service.

   systemctl restart nfs.service

5. n/a

6. Mount your share to test.

   mkdir /mnt/packages

   mount 172.18.0.50:/var/www/html/packages /mnt/packages

7. Share the /home directory as read/write to the local network.

   a. Edit the /etc/exports file to add the share.

      /home 172.18.0.0/24(rw,sync)

   b. Refresh the export list.

      exportfs -r

   c. Test your new share.

      mkdir /mnt/home

      mount 172.18.0.50:/home /mnt/home

8.–10. n/a

Chapter 23, Lab 1: Connecting to Existing Samba Shares (15–25 minutes)

Learning Objectives and Outcomes:

You will configure a client to connect to CIFS (Samba) shares.

Required Setup and Tools:

- Fedora Linux 15 installation with an ordinary user (student) and the root password

- Access to the classroom server Samba shares including username and password

- Access to the Fedora installation DVD or DVD ISO image file to install required packages

Additional Resources:

- Sobell, Chapter 23

Recommended Procedures:

1. Ensure that the Samba client tools are installed.

   Samba-client, i686

2. Browse the classroom server for available Samba shares from the command line.

   a. You do not require a password to connect as the Anonymous user: When you are prompted for a password, simply press RETURN.

      server faild

   b. Note the available public shares and printers.

   c. To connect as **mark** use the password **password**.

   d. Note the additional home directory share for mark.

3. Connect to the public Samba share using

   a. The Nautilus file browser

   b. The smbclient utility uses many of the same commands as an FTP client. Use **ls**, **cd**, **get**, and **put** to manage files.

c.   The **mount.cifs** command is equivalent to the **mount -t cifs** command and adds a Samba share to the local directory tree.

DELIVERABLES:

A system acting as a client to a remote Samba share.

CHAPTER 23, LAB 1—SOLUTIONS:

1. Ensure that the Samba client tools are installed.

   yum list samba-client

2. Browse the classroom server for available Samba shares from the command line.

   a. You do not require a password to connect as the Anonymous user: When you are prompted for a password, simply press RETURN.

   smbclient -L server

   b. Note the available public shares and printers.

   Varies: the file share named public should be visible and a printer share named foobar may be also be available.

   c. To connect as **mark** use the password **password**.

   smbclient -L server -U mark

   d. Note the additional home directory share for mark.

   In addition to the browsable shares found in step b, a share named mark should also be visible.

3. Connect to the public Samba share using

   a. The Nautilus file browser

   Places à Connect to Server
   Select Windows Share from the type pull down menu
   Fill in the server name (server.example.com) and share name (public)
   Connect as mark with a password of password
   The domain is mygroup

   b. The smbclient utility uses many of the same commands as an FTP client. Use **ls**, **cd**, **get**, and **put** to manage files.

   smbclient //server.example.com/public -U mark
   smbclient //server.example.com/mark -U mark

   c. The **mount.cifs** command is equivalent to the **mount -t cifs** command and adds a Samba share to the local directory tree.

   mkdir /smbshare
   mount.cifs -o user=mark //server.example.com/public /smbshare

CHAPTER 23, LAB 2: SHARING LOCAL DIRECTORIES USING SAMBA (20–30 MINUTES)

LEARNING OBJECTIVES AND OUTCOMES:

You will configure a server to use Samba for LAN file sharing.

REQUIRED SETUP AND TOOLS:

- Fedora Linux 15 installation with an ordinary user (student) and the root password

- Access to the classroom server Samba shares including username and password

- Access to the Fedora installation DVD or DVD ISO image file to install required packages

ADDITIONAL RESOURCES:

- Sobell, Chapter 23

RECOMMENDED PROCEDURES:

1. Working with root privileges, install the required packages.

2. Enable the services to start at boot time.

3. Start the smb and nmb services.

4. Add a Samba password for **mark** and **max**.

5. Browse the automatic printer shares (connect as the Anonymous user).

6. Browse the automatic home directory share (requires authentication).

7. Add a new share allowing public read-only access to the /tmp directory.

8. Troubleshooting: Check that the firewall is disabled or the CIFS port (445) is open.

9. Troubleshooting: Use **testparm** to check the configuration file syntax.

10. Modify the share to meet the following criteria:

    a. Share the /tmp/shared directory.

    b. Call the share **West**.

    c. Allow anyone to read the share.

    d. Allow the members of the group named **staff** to write to the share.

    e. Do not display the share in the browse list.

Deliverables:

A system acting as a Samba server for a read-only share and a share with selective write access.

CHAPTER 23, LAB 2—SOLUTIONS:

1. Working with root privileges, install the required packages.

   yum list samba*

   yum install samba

2. Enable the services to start at boot time.

   systemctl enable smb.service

   systemctl enable nmb.service

3. Start the smb and nmb services.

   systemctl start smb.service

   systemctl start nmb.service

4. Add a Samba password for **mark** and **max**.

   smbpasswd -a mark

   smbpasswd -a max

5. Browse the automatic printer shares (connect as the Anonymous user).

   smbclient -L localhost

6. Browse the automatic home directory share (requires authentication).

   smbclient -L localhost -U mark

   smbclient -L localhost -U max

7. Add a new share allowing public read-only access to the /tmp directory.

   [TEMP]

   comment = public share of /tmp

   path = /tmp

8. n/a

9. n/a

10. Modify the share to meet the following criteria:

    [West]

    comment = Files for the west wing staff

    path = /tmp/shared

    browseable = no

    write list = +staff

Chapter 23, Lab 3: Exploring SWAT (10–20 minutes)

Learning Objectives and Outcomes:

You will explore SWAT (the Samba Web Administration Tool).

Required Setup and Tools:

- Fedora Linux 15 installation with an ordinary user (student) and the root password

- Access to the classroom server SAMBA shares including username and password

- Access to the Internet to install required packages

Additional Resources:

- Sobell, Chapter 23, pages 830–834

Recommended Procedures:

If you have Internet connectivity, enable the Fedora repository and install the **samba-swat** package to explore the Samba Web Administration Tool (SWAT).

1. Back up the Samba config file.

2. Install the **swat** package and start the service.

3. Use SWAT to add a new share named **Press**, which shares the /tmp/press directory.

4. Save your configuration and restart the Samba server.

5. View config file. Note its similarity to the output of **testparm** and the lack of comments.

Deliverables:

A system acting as a Samba server for a share named Press.

CHAPTER 23, LAB 3—SOLUTIONS:

1. Back up the Samba config file.
    cp /etc/samba/smb.conf ~

2. Install the **swat** package and start the service
    yum - - enablerepo=fedora install samba-swat
    chkconfig swat on
    systemctl restart xinetd.service

3. Use SWAT to add a new share named **Press,** which shares the /tmp/press directory.
    mkdir /tmp/press
    cp /etc/hosts /tmp/press
    Use a Web browser (Firefox) to connect to http://localhost:901
    Use the links to add your share (Sobell, page 833, SHARES page)

4. Save your configuration and restart the Samba server.
    systemctl restart smb.service
    systemctl restart nmb.service

5. View config file. Note its similarity to the output of **testparm** and the lack of comments.
    diff ~/smb.conf /etc/samba/smb.conf
    cat /etc/samba/smb.conf
    testparm

Chapter 24, Lab 1: Exploring DNS Client Utilities (10–15 minutes)

Learning Objectives and Outcomes:

You will explore DNS client utilities.

Required Setup and Tools:

- Fedora Linux 15 installation with an ordinary user (student) and the root password

- Access to the Fedora installation DVD or DVD ISO image file to install required packages

- Access to the classroom server acting as a master nameserver for the example.com domain

Additional Resources:

- Sobell, Chapter 24

Recommended Procedures:

1. Modify the system to point to the classroom server for name resolution.

2. Use the **getent** utility to look up the IP address for server.example.com.

3. Use the **host** utility to look up the IP address for server.example.com.

4. Use the **dig** utility to look up the IP address for server.example.com.

5. Use the **host** utility to look up the name of 172.18.0.254.

6. Use the **dig** utility to look up the name of 172.18.0.254.

7. Use the **dig** utility to view the nameserver record for the example.com domain.

8. Use the **dig** utility to view the mail exchange record for the example.com domain.

Deliverables:

None

Chapter 24, Lab 1 — SOLUTIONS:

1. Modify the system to point to the classroom server for name resolution.
   Edit the /etc/resolv.conf file nameserver entry to look like the following:
   nameserver 172.18.0.254

2. Use the **getent** utility to look up the IP address for server.example.com.
   getent hosts server.example.com

3. Use the **host** utility to look up the IP address for server.example.com.
   host server.example.com

4. Use the **dig** utility to look up the IP address for server.example.com.
   dig server.example.com

5. Use the **host** utility to look up the name of 172.18.0.254.
   host 172.18.0.254

6. Use the **dig** utility to look up the name of 172.18.0.254.
   dig -x 172.18.0.254

7. Use the **dig** utility to view the nameserver record for the example.com domain.
   dig -t NS example.com

8. Use the **dig** utility to view the mail exchange record for the example.com domain.
   dig -t MX example.com

Chapter 24, Lab 2: Installing and Configuring a Caching-Only Nameserver (30–40 minutes)

Learning Objectives and Outcomes:

You will learn to configure a caching-only nameserver.

Required Setup and Tools:

- Fedora Linux 15 installation with an ordinary user (student) and the root password

- Access to the Fedora installation DVD or DVD ISO image file to install required packages

- Access to the classroom server acting as a master nameserver for the example.com domain

Additional Resources:

- Sobell, Chapter 24

Recommended Procedures:

1. Begin with JumpStart I (Sobell, page 860).

   a. Install the bind package from the DVD.

   b. Start the **named** daemon and set up **named** to start at boot time.

   c. Modify the /etc/resolv.conf file to use localhost (127.0.0.1) as your nameserver.

   d. If you have Internet access, look up the IP address of www.fedoraproject.org.

2. Issue the command **dig server.example.com**. Did dig display an IP address? Why or why not?

3. Add a forwarder entry that points to the classroom server.

   a. Add the following line to the **options** section of the /etc/named.conf:
   forwarders { 172.18.0.254; };

   b. Comment out the three **dnssec** lines in the **options** section.

   c. Restart the named service.

d. Troubleshooting: If the service fails to start, look for information in /var/log/messages and check the syntax of the lines you added to named.conf. You can also try issuing a stop command followed by a start command.

4. Look up the IP addresses of server.example.com and www.fedoraproject.org.

5. The default configuration listens only on the localhost interface. Configure your caching nameserver to answer queries for other systems.

   a. Edit the /etc/named.conf file and comment out the **listen-on** line in the **options** section.

   b. Edit the /etc/named.conf file and comment out the **allow-query** line in the **options** sections.

   c. Restart the named service.

6. Test: Change your /etc/resolv.conf file to point to your eth0 address 172.18.0.50. Lookup server.example.com and www.fedoraproject.org.

7. Troubleshooting: Restart the named service and look at the messages in the /var/log/messages file (Sobell, page 878).

8. Troubleshooting: Ensure that SELinux is in permissive mode (Sobell, page 462).

9. Troubleshooting: Ensure that the firewall is disabled or the named ports (tcp/53 and udp/53) are open (Sobell, page 893).

DELIVERABLES:

A caching-only nameserver.

CHAPTER 24, LAB 2—SOLUTIONS:

1. Begin with JumpStart I (Sobell, page 860).

   a. Install the bind package from the DVD.
      yum install bind

   b. Start the **named** daemon and set up **named** to start at boot time.
      systemctl start named.service
      systemctl enable named.service

   c. Modify the /etc/resolv.conf file to use localhost (127.0.0.1) as your nameserver.
      nameserver 127.0.0.1

   d. If you have Internet access, look up the IP address of www.fedoraproject.org.
      dig www.fedoraproject.org

2. Issue the command **dig server.example.com**. Did dig display an IP address? Why or why not?
   Without having an answer locally, the default configuration next looks to the Internet root servers. No lookups are directed to server.example.com and that is the only nameserver that has an IP assignment for the nameserver.example.com.

3. Add a forwarder entry that points to the classroom server.

   a. n/a

   b. n/a

   c. Restart the named service.
      systemctl restart named.service

   d. Troubleshooting: If the service fails to start, look for information in /var/log/messages and check the syntax of the lines you added to named.conf. You can also try issuing a stop command followed by a start command.
      systemctl stop named.service
      systemctl start named.service

4. Look up the IP addresses of server.example.com and www.fedoraproject.org.
   host server.example.com
   host www.fedoraproject.org

5. The default configuration listens only on the localhost interface. Configure your caching nameserver to answer queries for other systems.

   a. n/a

   b. n/a

   c. Restart the named service.
      systemctl restart named.service

6. Test: Change your /etc/resolv.conf file to point to your eth0 address 172.18.0.50. Lookup server.example.com and www.fedoraproject.org.

   nameserver 172.18.0.50

7.–9. n/a

CHAPTER 24, LAB 3: CONFIGURING A NAMESERVER AS A SLAVE SERVER (20–30 MINUTES)

LEARNING OBJECTIVES AND OUTCOMES:

You will learn configure a slave nameserver.

REQUIRED SETUP AND TOOLS:

- Fedora Linux 15 installation with an ordinary user (student) and the root password

- Access to the Fedora installation DVD or DVD ISO image file to install required packages

- Access to the classroom server acting as a master nameserver for the example.com domain

ADDITIONAL RESOURCES:

- Sobell, Chapter 24

RECOMMENDED PROCEDURES:

1. Preparation: View the contents of the /var/named/slaves directory and verify that you can look up an IP address for server.example.com.

2. Add a zone entry to the /etc/named.conf file to act as a slave nameserver for the example.com domain.

3. Check your syntax using the command named-checkconf /etc/named.conf

4. Restart the named service.

5. Test: View the contents of the /var/named/slaves directory and verify that you can lookup an IP address for server.example.com.

6. Add a zone entry to the /etc/named.conf file to act as a slave nameserver for the reverse lookup zone 0.18.172.in-addr.arpa domain.

7. Check the syntax, restart the service, and test your configuration.

DELIVERABLES:

A nameserver acting as a slave for the forward and reverse example.com domains defined on server.example.com.

CHAPTER 24, LAB 3—SOLUTIONS:

1. Preparation: View the contents of the /var/named/slaves directory and verify that you can look up an IP address for server.example.com.

   ls /var/named/slaves

   host server.example.com

2. Add a zone entry to the /etc/named.conf file to act as a slave nameserver for the example.com domain.

   zone "example.com" IN {

          type slave;

          masters { 172.18.0.254; };

          file "slaves/example.slave";

   };

3. n/a

4. Restart the named service.

   systemctl restart named.service

5. Test: View the contents of the /var/named/slaves directory and verify that you can lookup an IP address for server.example.com.

   ls /var/named/slaves

   host server.example.com

6. Add a zone entry to the /etc/named.conf file to act as a slave nameserver for the reverse lookup zone 0.18.172.in-addr.arpa domain.

   zone "0.18.172.in-addr.arpa" IN {

          type slave;

          masters { 172.18.0.254; };

          file "slaves/172.18.0.slave";

   };

7. Check the syntax, restart the service, and test your configuration.

   named-checkconf /etc/named.conf

   systemctl restart named.service

   ls /var/named/slaves

   host 172.18.0.254

Chapter 24, Lab 4: Configuring a Master Nameserver for a New Domain (20–30 minutes)

Learning Objectives and Outcomes:

You will learn configure a master nameserver.

Required Setup and Tools:

- Fedora Linux 15 installation with an ordinary user (student) and the root password

- Access to the Fedora installation DVD or DVD ISO image file to install required packages

Additional Resources:

- Sobell, Chapter 24

Recommended Procedures:

1. Add a zone definition for a master nameserver answering queries for the class.example.com subdomain.

2. Check your configuration using **named-checkconf**.

3. Create the zone file for the class.example.com domain. It should include

   a. A global time to live of 1 day

   b. An SOA record

   c. An NS record

   d. An MX record

   e. At least 3 A records

   f. At least 1 CNAME record

4. Check your zone file using **named-checkzone**.

5. Restart the named service and test using queries.

DELIVERABLES:

A master nameserver for the class.example.com domain.

CHAPTER 24, LAB 4—SOLUTIONS:

1. Add a zone definition for a master nameserver answering queries for the class.example.com subdomain.

   zone "class.example.com" IN {

   type master;

   file "class.zone";

   };

2. Check your configuration using **named-checkconf.**

   named-checkconf /etc/named.conf

3. Create the zone file for the class.example.com domain. It should include:

   a. A global time to live of 1 day

      $TTL 1D

   b. An SOA record

      class.example.com. IN SOA class.example.com. root.localhost. (

      1 ; serial

      1D ; refresh

      1H ; retry

      1W ; expire

      3H ; minimum

)

   c. An NS record

      class.example.com. NS   linux.class.example.com

   d. An MX record

      class.example.com. MX   10 linux.class.example.com.

   e. At least 3 A records

      grape.class.example.com.   A   172.18.0.55

      speedy.class.example.com. A   172.18.0.56

      peach.class.example.com.   A   172.18.0.57

   f. At least 1 CNAME record

      www.class.example.com.   CNAME   linux.class.example.com.

4. Check your zone file using **named-checkzone.**

   named-checkzone class.example.com /var/named/class.zone

5. Restart the named service and test using queries.

   systemctl restart named.service

   host www.class.example.com

Chapter 25, Lab 1: Enabling the Firewall Using the system-config-firewall Utility (10–15 minutes)

Learning Objectives and Outcomes:

You will use the graphical system-config-firewall utility to configure the kernel-based packet filtering firewall.

Required Setup and Tools:

- Fedora Linux 15 installation with an ordinary user (student) and the root password.

- Sobell Chapter 25, page 893, JumpStart

- Optional: Access to the classroom server to use as a client for testing.

Additional Resources:

- Sobell, Chapter 25, pages 892–895

Recommended Procedures:

1. Use the Firewall Configuration window to enable the firewall.

2. Ensure that the trusted services include sshd, ipp, and smb.

3. Apply your changes.

4. Test your configuration. If available, use the classroom server as your client.

   a. Can a client **ping** your system?

   b. Can a client use **ssh** to log in on your system?

   c. Can a client connect to your Samba shares?

   d. Can you still access the NFS shares and Web pages of another system?

   e. What is the output when a client issues the command **telnet 172.18.0.50 25**?

Explore the resulting configuration and view the loaded configuration from the command line.

5. View the /etc/sysconfig/iptables file.

6. Use the command line to view the current packet filtering configuration.

DELIVERABLES:

A system with the firewall enabled but allowing select configured services for select networks.

Chapter 25, Lab 1—SOLUTIONS:

1. Use the Firewall Configuration window to enable the firewall.

   Applicationsà Otherà Firewall

   or

   system-config-firewall

2. n/a

3. n/a

4. Test your configuration. If available, use the classroom server as your client.

   a. Can a client **ping** your system?

      Yes

   b. Can a client use **ssh** to log in on your system?

      Yes

   c. Can a client connect to your Samba shares?

      Yes

   d. Can you still access the NFS shares and Web pages of another system?

      Yes

   e. What is the output when a client issues the command **telnet 172.18.0.50 25**?

      No Route to Host

Explore the resulting configuration and view the loaded configuration from the command line.

5. View the /etc/sysconfig/iptables file.

   cat /etc/sysconfig/iptables

   The output is described in Sobell, page 909.

6. Use the command line to view the current packet filtering configuration.

   iptables -L

Chapter 25, Lab 2: Adding Packet Filtering Rules Using iptables (30–40 minutes)

Learning Objectives and Outcomes:

You will use the **iptables** utility to configure the kernel-based packet filtering firewall.

Required Setup and Tools:

- Fedora Linux 15 installation with an ordinary user (student) and the root password

- Optional: Access to the classroom server to use as a client for testing

Additional Resources:

- Sobell, Chapter 25

Recommended Procedures:

1. From the command line, insert a rule to accept SMTP packets (port 25) as used by sendmail.

2. Return to your client system (the classroom server). What does the command **telnet 172.18.0.50 25** display?

3. View your configuration.

   a. On your system, does your rule appear in the output of **iptables -L**?

   b. Does your rule appear in the /etc/sysconfig/iptables file?

   c. Reboot the system and retest.

4. From the command line, again add your rule to allow SMTP traffic. After testing your configuration, ensure that the rule remains in place after a reboot.

5. Modify the configuration file and apply the changes.

   a. Edit the /etc/sysconfig/iptables file to add rules to allow portmap (TCP port 111) and NFS traffic (TCP and UDP port 2049).

   b. Do your new rules appear in the output of **iptables -L**?

   c. How can you apply these rules without rebooting?

6. Explore the effect of the order of the rules.

    a. Find the line in the /etc/sysconfig/iptables that allows all new ssh traffic.

    b. Add a line just below that line that blocks ssh traffic only from the classroom server (172.18.0.254).

    c. Test that you can use ssh to log in on the classroom server. Which rule allows this connection?

    d. From the classroom server, can you **ping** your system? Which rule allows this connection?

    e. From the classroom server, can you ssh back to your system? Which rule allows this connection?

    f. Move the new rule so it is before the line that allows all ssh traffic and retest.

7. Cleanup: Remove the rule that blocks ssh traffic from the classroom server.

DELIVERABLES:

A system with the firewall enabled but allowing select configured services for select networks.

CHAPTER 25, LAB 2—SOLUTIONS:

1. From the command line, insert a rule to accept SMTP packets (port 25) as used by sendmail.
   iptables -I INPUT -p tcp --dport 25 -j ACCEPT

2. Return to your client system (the classroom server). What does the command
   telnet 172.18.0.50 25 display?
   If the server is running, it displays a welcome message from sendmail. Type quit to close the connection.

3. View your configuration.

   a. On your system, does your rule appear in the output of **iptables -L**?
      Yes, it should be the first rule.

   b. Does your rule appear in the /etc/sysconfig/iptables file?
      No

   c. Reboot the system and retest.
      The rule should have been cleared with a reboot. The telnet command should give a no route to host message. The rule should not appear in the output of iptables -L or in the file.

4. From the command line, again add your rule to allow SMTP traffic. After testing your configuration, ensure that the rule remains in place after a reboot.
   iptables -I INPUT -p tcp --dport 25 -j ACCEPT

   service iptables save
   or
   iptables-save > /etc/sysconfig/iptables

5. Modify the configuration file and apply the changes.

   a. n/a

   b. Do your new rules appear in the output of **iptables -L**?
      No

   c. How can you apply these rules without rebooting?
      systemctl restart iptables.service

6. Explore the effect of the order of the rules.

   a. n/a

   b. Add a line just below that line that blocks ssh traffic only from the classroom server (172.18.0.254).
      iptables -s 172.18.0.254 -p tcp -m state - -state NEW -m tcp - -dport 22 -j REJECT
      systemctl restart iptables.service

   c. Test that you can use ssh to log in on the classroom server. Which rule allows this connection?
      This connection is allowed by the ESTABLISHED/RELATED rules.

d. From the classroom server, can you **ping** your system? Which rule allows this connection?
This connection is allowed by a default ICMP rule.

e. From the classroom server, can you ssh back to your system? Which rule allows this connection?
Yes. This connection is allowed by the rule that allows all ssh traffic.

f. Move the new rule so it is before the line that allows all ssh traffic and retest.
Now it should be blocked. First rule wins.

7. n/a

CHAPTER 26, LAB 1: INSTALLING THE APACHE WEB SERVER (15–20 MINUTES)

LEARNING OBJECTIVES AND OUTCOMES:

You will use the Apache Web server to provide Web services under Linux.

REQUIRED SETUP AND TOOLS:

- Fedora Linux 15 installation with an ordinary user (student) and the root password

- Access to the Fedora installation DVD or DVD ISO image file to install required packages

ADDITIONAL RESOURCES:

- Sobell, Chapter 26

RECOMMENDED PROCEDURES:

1. Install **httpd** for HTTP services and **mod_ssl** for HTTPS services.

2. Enable and start the **httpd** service.

3. Locate the default DocumentRoot for the configuration installed with Fedora 15.

    a. Use an rpm query to determine configuration files installed with the package.

    b. Search the configuration file for the DocumentRoot parameter.

4. Create an index.html file that contains your system hostname in the directory DocumentRoot points to.

5. Have the index.html include a link to show the contents of the /var/ftp/pub directory. Install the FTP server if necessary (Sobell, Chapter 19). (Hint: You can use a symbolic link in the DocumentRoot to provide access to the FTP content.)

6. Test: Ensure you can view your index.html page.

7. Test the encrypted connection: Use Firefox and accept the localhost self-signed certificate.

8. Challenge: Follow the steps in the text (pages 959–961) to generate a customized self-signed certificate.

DELIVERABLES:

A Web server using the default configuration with a custom index page.

CHAPTER 26, LAB 1—SOLUTIONS:

1. Install **httpd** for HTTP services and **mod_ssl** for HTTPS services.
   yum install mod_ssl httpd

2. Enable and start the **httpd** service.
   systemctl enable httpd.service
   systemctl start httpd.service

3. Locate the default DocumentRoot for the configuration installed with Fedora 15.

   a. Use an rpm query to determine configuration files installed with the package.
      rpm -qc httpd

   b. Search the configuration file for the DocumentRoot parameter.
      grep DocumentRoot /etc/httpd/conf/httpd.conf

4. Create an index.html file that contains your system hostname in the directory DocumentRoot points to.
   You can use a text editor to create the file or you can use the following command:
   echo '<H2>Welcome to linux.example.com</H2>' > /var/www/html/index.html

5. Have the index.html include a link to show the contents of the /var/ftp/pub directory. Install the FTP server if necessary (Sobell, Chapter 19). (Hint: You can use a symbolic link in the DocumentRoot to provide access to the FTP content.)
   Add the following line to the /var/www/html/index.html file:

   Additional files are available in the <a href="pub">pub</a> directory
   ln -s /var/ftp/pub /var/www/html/pub

6. Test: Ensure you can view your index.html page.
   elinks --dump http://linux.example.com

7. n/a

8. n/a

Chapter 26, Lab 2: Configuring a Virtual Host (20–30 minutes)

Learning Objectives and Outcomes:

You will set up a virtual host using the Apache Web server.

Required Setup and Tools:

- Fedora Linux 15 installation with an ordinary user (student) and the root password

- Access to the Fedora installation DVD or DVD ISO image file to install required packages

Additional Resources:

- Sobell, Chapter 26

Recommended Procedures:

1. The classroom DNS server contains an alias entry for www.example.com pointing to linux.example.com Verify this name resolution.

2. Define a virtual host block using name-based virtual hosting for the www.example.com Web pages (Sobell, page 953).

    a. The DocumentRoot should be /web/html and contain an index.html file that indicates the site being served.

    b. Specify separate log files.

    c. Scripts should be stored in /web/cgi-bin

3. Check the syntax of the configuration file using **apachectl configtest** or **service httpd configtest** (Sobell, page 956).

4. Restart the **httpd** daemon.

5. Test: Ensure that you can view your new page at http://www.example.com.

6. Troubleshooting: Can the user named **apache** read the contents of index.html file?

7. Troubleshooting: If you get a permission denied error when viewing the new page, check the SELinux configuration using one of the following methods:

   a. Check that SELinux is in permissive mode with the following command:
      setenfore permissive

   b. Check that the SELinux context on the file is correct using
      chcon -R --reference /var/www/html /web/html

8. What happens when you view http://linux.example.com?

9. Add a second virtual host container to access the /var/www/html document root.

10. View the default error page for file not found. Use a browser to attempt to access a page that does not exist such as http://linux.example.com/not-here.html.

11. Modify the configuration so that a customized error message is displayed if a file is not found on the linux.example.com server.

    a. Create a custom error message file /var/www/error.custom404.html with a custom message.

    b. Modify the linux.example.com virtual host so that is uses the customized error message file for files it cannot find.

    c. Test your configuration. Attempt to view a non-existent page on both the linux.example.com and www.example.com servers.

DELIVERABLES:

A Web server serving content for two web sites.

CHAPTER 26, LAB 2—SOLUTIONS:

1. The classroom DNS server contains an alias entry for www.example.com pointing to linux.example.com
    Verify this name resolution.
    host www.example.com

2. Define a virtual host block using name-based virtual hosting for the www.example.com Web pages
    (Sobell, page 953).
    Edit the /etc/httpd/conf/httpd.conf file and add at the bottom:
    NameVirtualHost 172.18.0.50:80
    <VirtualHost 172.18.0.50:80>
    ServerName www.example.com
    DocumentRoot /web/html
    ErrorLog logs/www-error.log
    CustomLog logs/www-access.log common
    ScriptAlias /cgi-bin/ /web/cgi-bin/
    </VirtualHost>

3. n/a

4. Restart the **httpd** daemon.
    systemctl restart httpd.service

5. Test: Ensure that you can view your new page at http://www.example.com.
    elinks --dump http://www.example.com

6. n/a

7. n/a

8. What happens when you view http://linux.example.com?
    You see the content of the www.example.com site. With name-based virtual hosting, Apache will not
    revert back to the general configuration file. All servers must be defined inside a virtual host container.

9. Add a second virtual host container to access the /var/www/html document root.
    <VirtualHost 172.18.0.50:80>
    ServerName linux.example.com
    DocumentRoot /var/www/html
    </VirtualHost>

10. n/a

11. Modify the configuration so that a customized error message is displayed if a file is not found on the linux.example.com server.

    a. Create a custom error message file /var/www/error.custom404.html with a custom message.

    echo "custom error" > /var/www/error.custom404.html

    b. Modify the linux.example.com virtual host so that is uses the customized error message file for files it cannot find.

    Add a line:

    ErrorDocument 404 "/error/custom404.html"

    c. n/a

Chapter 26, Lab 3: Managing User Content and Private Directories (30–40 minutes)

Learning Objectives and Outcomes:

You will use the Apache Web server to provide Web services under Linux.

Required Setup and Tools:

- Fedora Linux 15 installation with an ordinary user and the root password

- Access to the Fedora installation DVD or DVD ISO image file to install required packages

Additional Resources:

- Sobell, Chapter 26

Recommended Procedures:

1. Enable the UserDir directive (Sobell, page 929) and uncomment the directory container for /home/*/public_html.

2. Create a ~max/public_html directory that includes an index.html file containing Max's name. Max should own the directory and have permission to modify the contents of the directory.

3. Change the permissions of /home/max and his public_html tree so Apache can read the content.

4. Restart the service and test.

5. Troubleshooting: SELinux may block the server's access to home directories. Ensure that SELinux is in permissive mode by giving the command **setenforce permissive** or use the command **setsebool -P httpd_enable_homedirs on** to change the SELinux Boolean settings.

6. Max wants to share some family photos, but only with a few relatives.

    a. Working as Max, create the ~/public_html/photos folder and add a file to the folder.

    b. Set the permissions so Apache can read the files.

    c. Create the ~/public_html/photos/.htaccess file to grant permission to any valid user (Sobell, pages 924 and 961). Store the passwords in a ~/.htpasswd file.

d.   Set up a ~/.htpasswd file for the user named **gramps** with a password of **password**.

e.   Test: Try to view the file you created in Max's photos directory.

DELIVERABLES:

A Web server offering users a place to offer personal content with password-protected content.

CHAPTER 26, LAB 3—SOLUTIONS:

1. Enable the UserDir directive (Sobell, page 929) and uncomment the directory container for /home/*/public_html.

   Edit the /etc/httpd/conf/httpd.conf file and comment out the UserDir disabled line and uncomment the UserDir public_html line.

2. Create a ~max/public_html directory that includes an index.html file containing Max's name. Max should own the directory and have permission to modify the contents of the directory.

   su – max

   mkdir ~/public_html

   echo max > ~/public_html/index.html

   exit

3. Change the permissions of /home/max and his public_html tree so Apache can read the content.

   chmod 755 ~max ~max/public_html

   chmod 644 ~max/public_html/*

4. Restart the service and test.

   systemctl restart httpd.service

   elinks --dump http://linux.example.com/~max

5. n/a

6. Max wants to share some family photos, but only with a few relatives.

   a. Working as Max, create the ~/public_html/photos folder and add a file to the folder.

      mkdir ~/public_html/photos

      touch ~/public_html/photos/somefile

   b. Set the permissions so Apache can read the files.

      chmod 755 ~/public_html/photos

   c. Create the ~/public_html/photos/.htaccess file to grant permission to any valid user (Sobell, pages 924 and 961). Store the passwords in a ~/.htpasswd file.

      AuthUserFile /home/max/.htpasswd

      AuthName "Private Photos"

      AuthType basic

      require valid-user

   d. Set up a ~/.htpasswd file for the user named **gramps** with a password of **password**.

      htpasswd -c ~/.htpasswd gramps

   e. n/a